# Passing the ICT Skills Test

## Fourth edition

# Passing the ICT Skills Test

## Fourth edition

Clive Ferrigan

LearningMatters

First published in 2001 by Learning Matters Ltd
Reprinted in 2002
Reprinted in 2003
Reprinted in 2004 (twice)
Second edition 2005
Reprinted in 2005
Reprinted in 2006
Reprinted in 2007
Third edition 2008
Reprinted in 2009 (twice)
Fourth edition 2011

British Library Cataloguing in Publication Data
A CIP record for this book is available from the British Library.

ISBN 978 0 85725 256 2

Adobe ebook ISBN 978 0 85725 258 6
EPUB ebook ISBN 978 0 85725 257 9
Kindle ISBN 978 0 85725 259 3

Cover design by Topics – The Creative Partnership
Text design by Code 5 Design Associates Ltd
Project Management by Deer Park Productions, Tavistock
Typeset by PDQ Typesetting Ltd, Newcastle-under-Lyme
Printed and bound in Great Britain by Bell & Bain Ltd, Glasgow

Learning Matters Ltd
20 Cathedral Yard
Exeter EX1 1HB
Tel: 01392 215560
info@learningmatters.co.uk
www.learningmatters.co.uk

**Mixed Sources**
Product group from well-managed forests and other controlled sources
www.fsc.org Cert no. TT-COC-002769
© 1996 Forest Stewardship Council
FSC

# Contents

# Acknowledgements

The publishers would like to thank the TDA for permission to use the screen shots on pages 3, 4 and 65–73. These screen shots have been taken from the practice ICT Skills Test on the TDA website www.tda.gov.uk and are the copyright of the Training and Development Agency for Schools.

The glossary is also reproduced courtesy of the TDA© Training and Development Agency for Schools. Permission to reproduce TDA copyright material does not extend to any material which is identified as being the copyright of a third party or to any photographs. Authorisation to reproduce such material would need to be obtained from the copyright holders.

# Series introduction

## The QTS skills tests

From 1 September 2008, all new trainee teachers will only be awarded QTS status if they successfully pass the skills tests. This removes the 'five-year grace period', which previously enabled trainees to practise as unqualified teachers without completing the skills tests for up to five years. All new entrants into the teaching profession in England will now have to pass the skills tests to be eligible for the award of QTS, including those on School Centred Initial Teacher Training and Graduate and Registered Teacher Programmes (GRTP).

The three tests cover skills in:

- **numeracy;**
- **literacy;**
- **information and communication technology (ICT).**

The tests will demonstrate that you can apply these skills to the degree necessary for their use in your day-to-day work in a school, rather than the subject knowledge required for teaching. The tests are taken online by booking a time at a specified centre, are marked instantly and your result, along with feedback on that result, will be given to you before you leave the centre.

You can find more information about the skills tests and the specified centres on the Training and Development Agency for Schools (TDA) website: *www.tda.gov.uk*

## Titles in this series

This series of books is designed to help you become familiar with the skills you will need to pass the tests and to practise questions on each of the topic areas to be tested.

**Passing the Numeracy Skills Test (fourth edition)**
Mark Patmore
ISBN 978 1 84445 169 2

**Passing the Literacy Skills Test (second edition)**
Jim Johnson
ISBN 978 1 84445 167 8

**Passing the ICT Skills Test (fourth edition)**
Clive Ferrigan
ISBN 978 0 85725 256 2

*To order, please contact our distributors:*
BEBC Distribution, Albion Close, Parkstone, Poole BH12 3LL
Tel: 0845 230 9000  Email: learningmatters@bebc.co.uk

# Introduction

## Why have an ICT skills test?

There is a growing recognition that the ability to use ICT (Information and Communications Technology) is now fundamental for the society in which we live. It is therefore not surprising that the government has taken the view that all teachers must have the skills to use ICT to support their work.

It is important to make a distinction here between the use of ICT to support the professional work of teachers and teaching the curriculum using ICT to enhance learning and achievement. The latter will come from your course and you will get opportunities to apply the skills you learn in the classroom.

The test does not test your ability to teach ICT or use it in subject teaching – it is purely a simple test to ensure that you know your way around a computer, the desktop and a variety of common applications.

## What ICT skills will the test cover?

The areas of ICT that will be tested are:

- **word processing;**
- **spreadsheets;**
- **e-mail;**
- **web browser;**
- **presentation software.**

(Note: the original test included the use of a database. This is no longer in the test; however, the section in this book on databases provides useful information for developing this area of your ICT skills.)

## Will I be expected to be an ICT expert before I can pass this test?

No! The test covers very basic competency. If you use a computer regularly then you should have no trouble.

However, there might be some applications which you have not used, or have used infrequently, which need to be part of your computer skills. While many of you will have used word processing, web browser and e-mail applications, you might have had less opportunity to use spreadsheets and databases.

## How will this book help me?

This book is intended to support you as you prepare to take the TDA ICT skills test. It is not a manual for all the applications (if it were, you would not be able to carry it around!).

It covers all the basic skills you will require for the test. In some cases it adds additional information in order that you can practise your skills. For example, you will not be expected to set up a database in the test but the book covers this briefly, so that you can set up a test database on which you can practise.

It is important not to be over confident because you are a regular user of a computer. Use this book to check that you are up to date with your skills. If something comes up in the test that you have not used before, then you might be in difficulty.

The test is timed – you will have 35 minutes. This will be plenty of time for someone who is prepared, but will pass far too quickly for someone who is struggling with his or her ICT skills.

The secret is to practise all the skills and make sure they become second nature. They are very common skills and you will use them whenever you use these applications, so the practice will not be wasted.

# How can I practise?

The test uses a generic set of tools. It uses a simple icon toolbar and menu structure. The tool options it provides are common to all the most popular applications. You should have no difficulty working through the test irrespective of the application with which you practised.

Obviously the most common suite of applications is Microsoft's Office. It does not matter which version you use, as the skills in the test are very basic and can be practised with any version.

If you cannot get access to Microsoft Office try Open Office from Sun Microsystems. This is a free alternative to Microsoft Office. It covers a large percentage of the functionality of Microsoft Office and will of course read files from Microsoft Office, and can save files in a variety of formats.

If you require Microsoft Office for your personal use then you can get it at a lower cost by obtaining an Academic Licence version. When you buy this version you get an empty box with a series of short forms. Fill these in, get your college to stamp the form to confirm your educational status and post them off to the address that is shown on the forms. A CD ROM will then be sent to you.

If you buy a new computer it will often come with an office suite of some kind. Another source of slightly older, but virtually free, applications are the computer magazines' free discs. They often have an older version of an office suite as a give-away on the CD ROM. Do not expect versions of Microsoft Office to come through this route.

# What about the look of the desktop? Will I be able to find my way around?

The test is designed to have the common feel of a Windows environment. It is easy to use and uncluttered, so you will not have to search for an application. All the applications can be opened from an icon on the desktop and there is also a folder on the desktop, which contains the files you will need.

**Note**: *Unfortunately, the test environment does not support either 'right click' menus or keyboard short cuts. However, you can mark and copy text from emails, web sites, etc. using copy/paste functions in the tool bar. This saves time so use this where possible rather than type text in directly.*

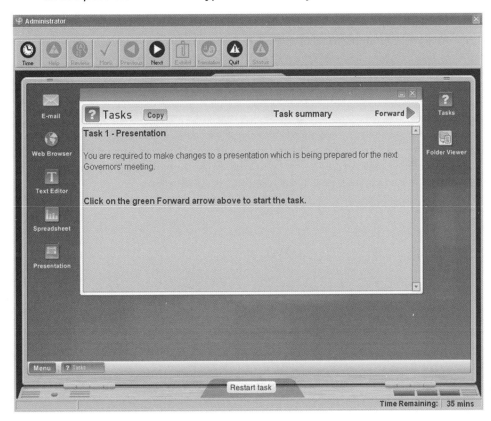

Application icons are on the left of the desktop and can be started by double clicking the icon.

Any open window will show as a button on the bar below the window (next to the green menu button). If you minimise a window then it can be opened again by clicking its button on this bar.

The screen above has the task window open. The task window takes you through the various tasks you will be asked to complete. Note the 'task' button next to the green 'menu' button which shows that this window is open.

The 'previous' and 'next' buttons on the menu bar allow you to move between tasks, although it is advisable to complete one task before moving on to the next.

Each task has six parts and, once the task is open, the 'forward' and 'back' buttons move you between the parts of that particular task.

On the right of the screen you can see two other icons. One opens the folder view. Here you can see the files that you will need to use for the task at hand. Double clicking the files will open the application as well. Files use different icons for each application, e.g. a 'T' for text file, a small image for a graphic file.

**Note:** *The folder will only contain the files you need when you reach that part of the task. They will not be available at other times (see chapter on Preparing for the test).*

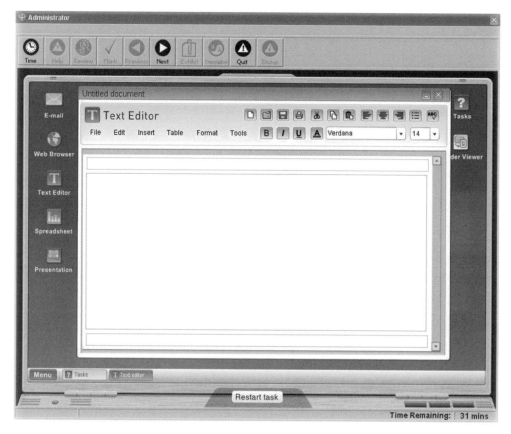

The screen above shows the Text Editor application open. The application menu structure will be looked at in the Preparing for the test chapter of this book.

The time remaining for the test is also shown bottom right. If this puts you off, then clicking on the time icon turns it off. However, I suggest you leave it on, as time (whilst using a computer) tends to run away.

Basically, managing the test environment is common sense.

# What will be the context of the test?

The test could have tested individual skills in isolation, e.g. write a letter, use a spreadsheet, etc. However, most sensibly, the test designers have chosen to simulate the use of ICT in a real situation.

So, in each test the individual tasks will be built around a specific context, e.g. preparing a presentation for a governors' meeting on a given topic. All activities are linked to the context given at the start of the task. You will be expected to move between applications and use a range of simple ICT skills to fulfil each task. For example, you might be required to take text from an e-mail and include this in a presentation and alter the font, etc. to meet requirements given in the e-mail. Check the online benchmark tests so that you are familiar with the different types of contexts used in the tests. Most tests will include at least one task with an 'e-safety' context.

You will find that you might have several applications open at the same time as well as the task instruction window. You can switch between each window quickly by clicking on the icon on the task bar at the bottom of the screen.

The exact activities and the context might change but the principle will remain the same. The contexts are intended to be familiar to both Primary and Secondary school environments.

# What is the structure of the test?

The test has a clear structure:

- **Welcome screen**
- **Introduction to the desktop**
- **Task context**
- **Task screens.**

> HINT In general, people do not read information off computer screens very carefully. They tend to be eager to move on or just gain a gist of what is being said. You, however, will need to read each screen carefully to ensure that you know what is required. For example, the introduction screen will give you the context of the test and the tasks you will be required to perform.

# What general computing skills do I need?

It is important that you know your way around a computer and the desktop and you need reasonable mouse and keyboard skills.

You do not need to be a touch typist but your text entry needs to be accurate.

Here are some of the most commonly needed skills, with a quick reminder about how to use them. Remember this is not a manual and if you need to go further then any quick guide to the Windows Operating System will help.

You need to be able to:

**Open an application from an icon on the desktop and close an application when you have finished**. The simplest way to do this, and the method used in the test, is to double click on the application's icon with the left-hand button of the mouse. In Windows 98, 2000, XP and Vista you can use the Start button (bottom left of the desktop), go to Programs and move down until you find your application and click once. To close an application, simply click on the ⊠ button at the top right-hand corner of the application.

**Use the mouse to drag and drop files, etc.** Click on a file or object with the left-hand mouse button to select it, keep the button held down and drag the file or object to where you want it to go. Practise this by dragging files from a USB drive to a folder on the hard drive and by moving a graphic around a document.

**Open two applications at the same time and size the windows so that both can be viewed, e.g. a word processor and Internet Explorer to allow you to copy and paste information from the Internet into your document**. To do this you click on your first application's icon and open it, then do the same for your second application. You then need to move your applications' windows around a bit so that you can see both applications at the same time.

Above are the window control buttons. The top three buttons control the application window and the bottom button will close the current document or image. You need to know how to work with these buttons.

The first of the row of three is the minimise button. This will shrink your application window to an icon on the task bar at the bottom of your screen. Remember that your application is still running. This is useful when you want to go to use another application temporarily and then return to the original one. Computers that do not have sufficient memory will slow down alarmingly as you open more than one application. Even 512 Mb is now considered borderline for efficient running of two applications at the same time.

The second button is the one that allows you to move and resize a window. If it looks like the one in the left-hand image then the window is maximised and cannot be moved or resized. If you click on this button it will change to look like the one in the middle of the three in the right-hand image. Now you can drag and resize the window. Click and hold the left-hand mouse button in the blue bar at the top of your window (if it is not blue then your window is not active so just click anywhere inside the window and the bar will change to blue as the window becomes active again). Now drag your window aside. You will see the desktop beneath it.

Go to any corner or edge and you will see the mouse pointer change to look like this

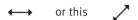

or this

You can then use your mouse to drag the edges or the corners of your window to resize it. When it is the size that you want, you can then do the same to your other application. This way you can see both open at the same time.

Note: *The test only uses the minimise and close buttons.*

**Find out information about a file, e.g. its size, whether it is read-only, etc.** This is easy. Go to the icon of the file you are interested in and right click the mouse button. A floating menu will appear. Go down to Properties and you will get an information box which will tell you the file's size, type and any other information, e.g. whether the file is read-only, etc. At this point you can also choose to make the file read-only. This is useful to protect your file from absent-minded misuse.

Another way of finding information about files is to go to Windows Explorer or to My Computer and open the drive (by clicking on it) and any folder that contains the file/files you want to investigate. Go to the menu at the top of the window and select **Views/Detail**. You will then see all files listed with details about them including file size and type.

Note    *File size is important if you are saving to a portable medium such as a USB pen drive. These have limited capacity. Modern applications, with a lot of graphics, can easily create large files. You sometimes need to know the size of your file in order to know whether it will fit in the available space.*

**Know a little about different file types and which applications will open them.** Mostly you rarely see the file extension even if you follow the procedure above. This is because Windows maintains a list of the file extensions and their associated applications or meanings. It then reads the extension and shows you to which program it belongs, e.g. instead of showing a .doc extension you would see 'word document'.

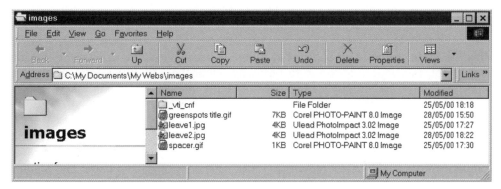

Above you can see a variety of file extensions and the associated type given by Windows. Where the type is a known type, e.g. jpeg (.jpg), Windows shows you the application that will open it.

Normally the file extensions are switched off. If you really want to know then go to **View/ Folder Options**, which will give you a floating dialogue box. Select the **View** tab and look for the option '**Hide file extensions for known file types**'. You will see the little box next to this is checked. Click here and uncheck the box in order to see the file extensions in the detailed list of files.

**Make selections by using the mouse buttons.** This is just a reminder that in many applications, on the desktop and in Windows showing files, you can click your left mouse button near the files you want and draw around them selecting them as a group. This feature is found in DTP packages for selecting a group of objects, etc. It's quite useful if you want to move a group of files or delete them.

**Be able to select, copy and paste text, using the clipboard, to transfer information between applications.** This is a 'must-have' skill. Anything you select with your mouse, be it a chunk of text in a document or an image from a web page, can be copied into the clipboard (this is just an area of memory put aside to hold copied items). To select text, place the cursor at the start of the text, hold down the left-hand button of the mouse and drag over the text you want to highlight. You can then paste the text or images back into another application. These cut, copy and paste tools are usually found in the **Edit** menu.

**Print a file, change the print quality if required, alter the number of copies and change the orientation of the page.** As you might imagine, this is a simple operation. You will find either a print icon or a menu selection to allow you to print from the application.

The menu selection is almost universally under **File/Print**. Be careful here as the operation of the icon can be different to the operation of the menu choice. The icon can quite often trigger an automatic print run of one copy using previous settings of the printer. If you need to alter the settings (e.g. the number of copies, quality, etc.) then use the menu option.

You will then get a print dialogue box. From here you can select various options. Notice that at the top of the dialogue box it tells you which printer it will be using. If you have more than one printer (on a network, for example) you can change the printer here.

Next to this is the Properties box for your selected printer. Clicking here will bring up options specific to the chosen printer.

**Use the Undo option in an application.** There is usually an Undo icon on the tool bar but, if not, the Undo function is to be found under the Edit menu option. This is a lifesaver. Some modern applications have multiple undoes, which can take you back many stages of alteration, and redoes to move you forward.

**Use the Preview option.** Most applications that can produce printed output also include a **Preview** option that will allow you to view each page as it will appear when printed. This is a very useful feature as it can save a lot of wasted paper and printing time. Always check the final look and fit of a page before you print.

If you are lucky enough to be using Office 2007 then you will be aware that the menu and tool bars are radically different in both their appearance and how you access them. Although they have the same functions as before it is still best that you practise on Office 2000, XP, 2003 or Open Office, as these use the familiar layout that is also used in the tests.

# 1 | Word processing

## Introduction

The skills to use a word processing program are now fundamental to the professional development of teachers. Walk into any school and you will find that the shift to the use of this technology has made a significant difference to the work of even the most diehard technophobe.

It is important for you to have the skills to take advantage of the text management and manipulation facilities offered by word processing. Your life as a teacher will be made so much easier, as you prepare materials for the children, work on planning documents, write letters to parents, etc., by the editing and storage functions of the word processor. No longer will whole pages of Schemes of Work, etc. have to be retyped to incorporate some small change.

The main word processing software used in schools is Microsoft Word. However, there are a range of office suites that include a range of word processors, e.g. Open Office, Corel Office and Star Office. Although not common, many of these offer almost all the functionality of Microsoft Word at a lower cost. It is worth remembering that Microsoft Word is an 'industrial strength' program which has some very advanced features – the majority of users only scratch the surface of its capabilities.

All these programs will save and load Word documents, provided they are of the correct version. What is important is that they have a range of common core features. The QTS test will be looking for you to have the skills to operate these common core features. The test will use a generic word processor that will look and feel like Word. There might be slight differences which, if you are not ready for them, could cause you to waste time searching for a specific tool. All word processors operating in the Windows environment use icons to give quick access to common features, with more advanced or less-used functions being found in the menu bar.

The Windows Operating System has ensured that all software has a common look and feel. In this section you will find examples from the toolbars of several word processors, emphasising their common features.

The QTS test is an online test of your skills. To pass this test you must have practised your skills and be certain you know how to perform all the functions mentioned in this chapter. Many of the skills you will already possess and use regularly in your work, but others might not be so common and you will need to refresh your memory.

The test is 35 minutes long and you will not have a lot of time to spare, so practice will ensure that you are up to speed and do not waste time.

## Word processing basic

Here is the main menu and tool bars for Microsoft Word. Most word processors (e.g. Open Office) look very similar.

It is useful to remember that functions you find in one program under one heading do not always appear in the same place in another program.

We have already covered the basic computing skills you will require. Here are the main core things you should be able to do with your text using a word processor.

# Basic operations

There will be many ways of achieving these operations but here are the most common.

**Note:** *When selecting an item from the menu bar it will either make something happen immediately, e.g. changing the page view, or it will produce a floating dialogue box for you to use. The icons provide fast access to specific functions. An example of this is the print icon in Word. This causes the document to be printed without any further input from you. However, if you choose Print from the File menu then you are offered choices through a dialogue box.*

**Inserting a character/word/sentence/paragraph or chunk of text**. This is very basic and involves moving the cursor to where you want to insert, clicking the left mouse button and typing. The body of the text will arrange itself in response to the additional text you are typing.

**Using the Undo command**. The most valuable tool. You can undo your mistakes! In older programs this would only 'undo' the last thing you did. However, now you have multiple 'undoes', which means you can recover text after several changes. Be careful as it does not always do what you expect and it is still possible to lose text even with this facility. Note that all the tool bars have an icon for this feature and it is also under the **Edit** menu.

Undo      Redo

**Inserting a special symbol**. You will find you will need this quite often to insert accents, copyright symbols, etc. Move to where you want the insertion and click the left mouse button to place the insertion cursor (like an I beam), go to the **Insert** menu and choose **Symbol**, choose the symbol you want and insert.

**Inserting a page break**. It is often useful to force a page to break where you want it rather than have a paragraph split over two pages. Place your cursor where you want the break and press **Ctrl** and **Enter** to insert the break.

**Selecting text**. This is easy but poor mouse skills can make it difficult to select a single letter, so practise. Selection is most commonly done by placing the cursor at the start of the text, holding down the left-hand button of the mouse and dragging over the text you want to highlight. In Word you can go to the left-hand margin of the text where the cursor changes to an arrow facing the text. Clicking here will select the whole line and, by moving down, the whole paragraph, etc.

*HINT*  The best way to select text accurately is to click at the start of the text you wish to select and then move the cursor to the end of the text, hold down the shift key and click again. This will then select all the text between the two points.

If you need to select all the text use the **Edit/Select All** menu option.

**Using copy and paste**. This allows you to duplicate text in different parts of the document. Select the text as above then press the **Copy** icon or select **Copy** from the **Edit** menu. Move the cursor to where you want the text and click the **Paste** icon or use **Paste** from the **Edit** menu.

Cut    Copy    Paste

*HINT*  Sometimes it is faster using the keyboard short cuts for particular functions. However, these are not always common across programs, so you will need to learn the most useful for the one you use, e.g. Ctrl+C copies the selected text and Ctrl+V pastes the text. Note the test does not allow keyboard short cuts. However, these are so useful it is worth acquiring the commonest ones.

**Copying or moving text between two open documents**. This is a very valuable skill. For example, you can have the National Curriculum subject document open in one window and your planning document in another. Extracts from the National Curriculum can be selected, copied and pasted into your document. To do this you open your first document using the file menu, then you open the second using the same menu. Move to the **Window** menu and select **Arrange all**. This will give you one document above another and you can then scroll through either and move or copy text backwards and forwards.

In later versions of Microsoft Office there is the 'Office Clipboard'; which is to be found under the **Edit** menu option. Using this allows you to copy several different parts of a document to the clipboard and paste them in any order to wherever you want them. It is a very useful function to learn but is not available in the test.

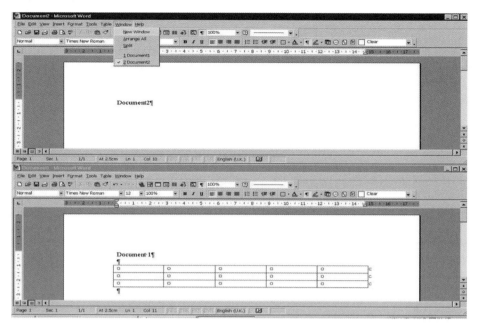

**Deleting text**. This is easy but make sure you know the effect of the delete key and backspace key. You can also select text and press delete. It is useful to know that if you select text and then start typing again the selected text will be deleted in favour of the new text being entered. This can save a bit of time.

**Find and replace**. Try to learn this, as it is useful for working on standard letters or placing information into the text that was not available at the time. You could, for instance, use the '@' sign where you want a child's name to be placed in a standard letter. Then using find and replace change the '@' to the child's name for all occurrences. This is usually found in the **Edit** menu.

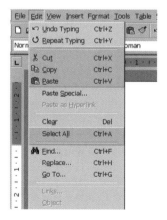

**Changing fonts: size, type, colour and weight**. You can select text and change this to bold, italics or underline using the icons on the toolbar. Most toolbars also show drop-down menus to select a different font for your selected text, and to change its size. These options are also available under the menu item **Format**.

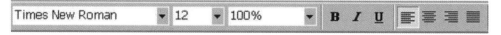

*HINT* The right-hand button of your mouse will also give you a range of options if you use it when you have clicked inside a body of text or selected some text. The options vary from program to program but give you quick access to commonly used items. The test does not use the functionality of the right click mouse button. However, copy, paste, cut, delete and select all (where applicable) are available from the tools menu at the top of an application in the test.

**Justifying text and aligning text**. There are usually icons associated with these functions. The example below shows the three usual icons on the end of the font formatting tools. Text can be aligned to the left or right margins and centred. Justifying a body of text gives it straight edges on both the left and right. This is achieved by the program adjusting the space between the words to achieve the justification; the result is that in some cases the spaces can be uneven and, occasionally, rather large. This is the effect you sometimes see in newspaper columns.

**Hyphenation and line spacing**. Hyphenation can be switched off and on for a paragraph. The controls for this are in the **Format** menu. In Word hyphenation is switched off and on in the **Format/Paragraph** dialogue box.

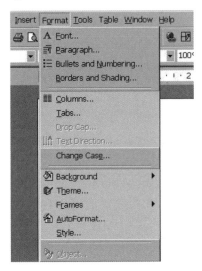

**Indenting text**. There are several routes to indenting a piece of text. This is a good skill to acquire as it allows you to make text more readable. It is also important for structured documents with numbered paragraphs and sub paragraphs, such as school policies, etc.

A simple way of indenting a paragraph is to mark it or click at the beginning of the paragraph and then click on the Indent icon. This moves the text to the next fixed tab point on the ruler. Clicking the icon again will indent one tab further.

Subsequent paragraphs will remain indented until you click on the reverse icon.

*HINT* When using the **indent** icons the text wraps to the new left-hand edge. When you press **Return** the cursor moves to the start of the next line in the same place as the indented text. These are called the wrap and return margins respectively. You need to know how to use these to lay out text more accurately.

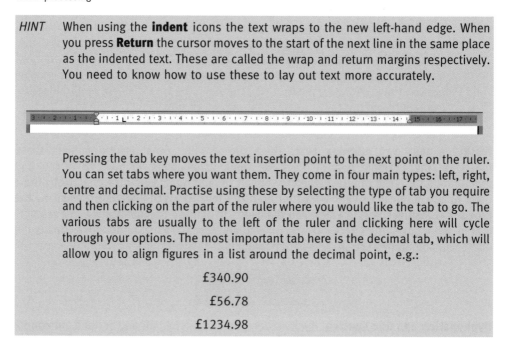

Pressing the tab key moves the text insertion point to the next point on the ruler. You can set tabs where you want them. They come in four main types: left, right, centre and decimal. Practise using these by selecting the type of tab you require and then clicking on the part of the ruler where you would like the tab to go. The various tabs are usually to the left of the ruler and clicking here will cycle through your options. The most important tab here is the decimal tab, which will allow you to align figures in a list around the decimal point, e.g.:

£340.90

£56.78

£1234.98

Unfortunately there are two more ways of indenting text. You can use the **Format/ Paragraph** menu. However, the best way of controlling the wrap and return margins is using the two buttons on the ruler (they look like two arrows on top of each other).

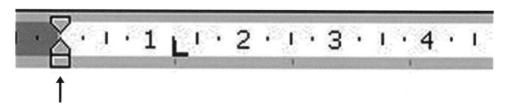

Clicking and dragging the small square at the bottom drags both arrows to where you want the paragraph to be indented.

Moving the top icon moves the return margin but not the wrap margin so that the first line is indented but the remaining text wraps to the left-hand margin. Like this!

Pressing return sends the cursor to the return margin position and this is in line with the first line of the paragraph above.

*HINT* You can move the bottom wrap margin independently of the top by holding down shift and then dragging. You can mark a paragraph and then drag the margin icons to move the paragraph to where you want it, e.g.:

100 Thistle Avenue

Aspley

Nottingham NG99 5ZZ

Here the address has been aligned right and produces the wrong result.

100 Thistle Avenue
Aspley
Nottingham NG99 5ZZ

Marking the address and moving both the margin icons places the address where you need it.

**Changing line spacing**. You might use this to allow children to write between lines of text or mark specific types of word, e.g. adjectives. Pressing return twice only works on single lines. To adjust line spacing in a paragraph you use the **Format/Paragraph** menu. You will then see a dialogue box to guide your choices.

**Bullets and numbered lists**. This can be done by clicking on the appropriate icons.

However, the results are sometimes unpredictable. You have greater control by going to the **Format/Bullets and Numbering** menu and working with the dialogue box. You will use this feature a lot; it is most useful in drawing attention to a series of short specific points.

**Page borders**. You can add a border to a whole page using the **Format/Borders** and **Shading** menu option.

**Using templates**. This is a common feature of word processors. Templates store a basic structure for a document and contain document settings such as fonts, key assignments, macros, menus, page layout, special formatting, and styles. There are several built-in templates for you to use, e.g. different styles of letter, fax pages, etc. Templates are a quick way of setting up a new document in a particular way. You can also set up your own document template but this is not likely to form part of the test.

> *HINT* It is worth designing your own templates for specific functions in your work, e.g. school reports, etc.

## *Using styles. This is a feature that allows you to apply different, pre-built, styles to a paragraph or word.*

The above paragraph was formatted using **Format/Style/Heading 5** in Word. These are occasionally useful for fast formatting. This is used in the test.

**Headers and footers**. These are essential. Learn them. They will help you keep track of documents and not get pages from a print-out muddled up. A policy document without page numbers annoys all those who have to read it – they have no reference point. Headers and footers can contain all sorts of text but the usual is the author, date and/or page number.

---

HINT *HINT*  Another useful header or footer is the file name and file path.

---

In Word the option is found under the **View/Header and Footer** menu option. You can toggle between the header and footer. When you become more expert you can use the section numbering, etc. which allows you to split your document into different sections and number these accordingly.

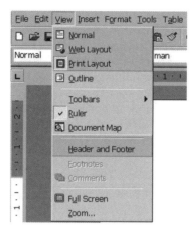

When you select this option a floating toolbar will appear with various icons which insert commonly used options, e.g. page number, date, etc. and a useful feature called Auto Text which has further options, e.g. file name and author, etc.

**Spell checking**. There is an icon for this or you can use the **Tools/Spelling and Grammar** menu option.

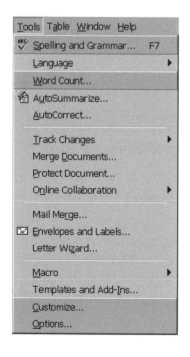

If you need to check a specific word, just highlight it and go to the spell checker.

Make sure your spell checker is set up for UK English and not US English, else you will have trouble with words like colour/color and centre/center.

**Changing page setup**. This allows you to choose between landscape and portrait, choose a basic size, e.g. A4, and set margins, etc. This is found in **File/Page Setup**. You will usually stick to A4 as a paper size but you will often find the margins are more generously set than you would wish.

**Note:** *Any changes you make apply to your whole document. However, if you use sections, it is possible to have a different page setup in each section. Thus you can mix portrait and landscape orientation in one document.*

**Using tables**. The ability to create tables is one of the most useful functions within a word processor. You must learn how to do this, as it will allow you to present information in a clear and organised manner. It will also allow you to create quite complex page layouts to hold information. It is unlikely that you will be asked to do more than create a simple table in the test.

Most word processors have an icon that will allow you to create a table very quickly.

The left-hand icon in this example creates the table. The next icon allows you to insert a spreadsheet. Interestingly, some spreadsheet functions are available in a table, e.g. SUM of cells.

Another route to creating a table is through the menu bar. The table item can be found under **Insert** or **Create** but in Microsoft Word it has its own menu **Table**.

| Spelling Test Scores | | | |
|---|---|---|---|
| *Child's name* | *29/09/00* | *06/10/00* | *13/10/00* |
| *Peter Piper* | *45%* | *67%* | *90%* |
| *Mary Moon* | *34%* | *56%* | *91%* |

By formatting the individual cells or rows or columns, quite complex layouts can be achieved. Notice that the title 'Spelling Test Scores' fits across the columns. This is done by merging the cells in that row.

The use of tables to create planning documents, development plans, audit forms, data collection sheets, etc. is now becoming commonplace and a necessary skill.

> **HINT** If the data you collect is going to be analysed statistically it might seem easier to create the collection form in Word. However, you can create the same style of tables in a spreadsheet such as Excel and this is a more appropriate program to actually work on the data.

The borders and shading of your table can be altered in a range of ways. This is usually a menu option either under **Table/Table Properties** or under **Format/Borders and Shading**.

> **HINT** Don't forget the right-hand mouse button. With many programs this will give you a short cut to options you need, e.g. if you click inside a table or select a whole table and then use the right-hand mouse button you will be offered a series of short cuts to appropriate menu options.

It is useful to remember that you can use the tables to create columns of related data and then remove the borders to make the columns appear neatly on the page. In the past this was only possible using complex tabbing. For example:

| Paragraph 6 Tables and their properties | Creating tables | Using the icon bar |  |
| | | | The left icon allows you to insert a table. |
| | | Using the menu bar | This is usually found under its own menu heading, etc. |
| | Formatting tables | Borders and shading | |

There is a lot more you can do with tables. You need to practise this skill and develop your expertise.

**Inserting an image**. Once again this is either through an icon or through the menu bar **Insert/Picture**.

The picture here was inserted from a file on a disc. It is in a **.jpg** (JPEG) format. This is the most usual format for a photograph. However, for clipart and some photographs the format can be one of many, e.g. **.gif, .wmf, .bmp, .tif**, etc.

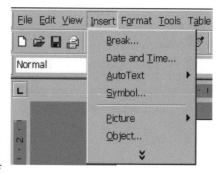

**Note:** *Each of these formats has specific properties which mean they might be compressed, or they are bitmap files which do not resize easily or they are vector formats which can be resized to almost any size without loss of detail, etc.*

Most word processors will take in a whole range of formats and this will be done without you having to make any decision. However, it is worth knowing a little about the graphics file formats as you can be offered different options for saving when you use a scanner or digital camera.

You will notice that in the example above the picture of the menu bar is mixed in with the text. This is a feature of the image  called 'text wrapping'. This means you can fix an image on the page, or allow it to float and be dragged to where you want it. It also allows you to position an image so that the text flows around the image.

In the above paragraph the text has not been centred as you might imagine, rather it has been placed in position by adjusting the left and right wrapping margins, justifying the text and then clicking on the picture and setting its text wrap properties to 'square'. To find the text wrap properties menu and other formatting features for the picture, first click on the picture and then go to **Format/Picture** or use the right-hand mouse button. (In Word clicking on a picture automatically brings up a floating toolbar.)

You will need to practise this to make sure you can easily insert graphics into your text from a variety of sources, e.g. a digital camera, scanner, clipart collection, etc.

**Moving and sizing graphics**. Graphics are normally associated with the text surrounding them and will move with this text. Like the text they can be centred, etc. However, if you need to move the graphic anywhere on the page then you will need to set the text wrapping to something such as 'tight' or 'through'. This will allow you to place the graphic anywhere on the screen and the text will then adjust itself automatically to the wrapping set for the image.

When you click on an image you will usually see a square appear around the image with eight smaller squares visible (called the sizing handles) – these are in each corner and in the middle of each side of the larger square. Move the cursor over these and you will see it change to two arrows. At this point holding down the left-hand mouse button and dragging will allow you to enlarge or reduce the size of the image.

It is very easy to alter the proportions of an image, as you can see from the above example. There are various ways to keep proportionality. You will need to find these out. However, the most common is to hold down the shift key while dragging from any of the corners – this will keep the whole image in proportion.

**Using drawing tools**. There is quite a range of drawing tools available in most word processors. These allow you to create quite complex diagrams, flow charts, etc. They are usually accessed through the icon tool bar. If they are not present then go to **View/ Toolbars** and select the drawing toolbar.

You will have to explore the range of options available but try and practise simple shapes and arrows.

> *HINT*   Have a look at **AutoShapes**. These produce a whole range of useful features such as call-out boxes, arrows, stars, etc. For example, this arrow:
>
>

**Using text boxes**. The drawing tools, images and text boxes allow you to use the word processor almost as a desk top publishing program. Text boxes are just boxes for entering text, and you can move them around the page, adjusting wrapping and place them inside other text, etc.

It is worth learning how to use text boxes. You can also add colour fills and borders, etc.

**Inserting files, spreadsheets, etc**. It is possible to create Excel spreadsheets within Word using the icon on the toolbar or the **Insert/Object/Microsoft Excel Worksheet** menu. You can also insert worksheets from the **Insert/File** menu. It is useful to be able to do this for reports, etc. You can also select sections of a spreadsheet and then **copy and paste** this into a document. It is also possible to dynamically link a spreadsheet in a document so that the data is updated automatically when the spreadsheet has been changed.

Other documents can be inserted in an open document. This is very useful when you have a series of smaller documents (e.g. created by different members of staff) that you want to build into one main document. Again you can do this through the **Insert/File** menu.

**Mailing lists and mail merge**. This is not likely to occur in the test. However, it is useful to know how to do this. Basically there are two actions you need to take. The first is to create the data file with the fields you might want to use, e.g.

| Title | First Name | Second Name | Address 1 | Address 2 | City | Post Code |
|---|---|---|---|---|---|---|
| Mr | John | Doe | 120 The Avenue | Grandy | Nottingham | NG36 4FH |
| Mrs | Helen | Smith | 132 The Avenue | Grandy | Nottingham | NG36 6FH |

As you can see, this is created in a table and the first row of the table shows the fields you wish to use.

The next thing to do is create a main letter that will contain the text you wish to send to everyone. Finally you merge the two documents by inserting the fields into the main document you will be using and then merging them. The computer then prints each document with the data for each person inserted in the correct places. Sounds hard!! It would be, but Word holds your hand as you do this and helps you all the way. You will find mail merge under **Tools/Mail Merge**.

The fields are placed in the main document between < <  > > markers, e.g.:

```
< <First Name> >   < < Second Name> >
< <Address1> >
< <Address2> >
< <City> >
< <Post Code> >

Dear  < <Title> >   < <Second Name> >

Thank you for your letter, etc. ...
```

Using the same data document you can also print mailing labels, etc. You will find these under **Tools/Envelopes and Labels**. Once again the program will take you through the necessary steps.

**Word count**. This is a useful feature for giving a quick idea of how many words you have used. This is often helpful when you are asked to produce a report of a certain length or a submission (e.g. for a grant) of restricted length. You will find this in **Tools/Word Count**.

**Compatibility**. Most versions of a word processor are upward compatible, but the same does not work in reverse. A document written in Word 6 or Word 95/97 can be read by Word 2000; but a Word 2000 document cannot be read by Word 95. This can be very important, especially when sending documents to other colleagues by e-mail. You cannot assume that they have the same program version as yours. Indeed they might not even have the same word processor.

The way around this is to send all documents in Word 6.0/95 format. This can be found in the **Save as** floating dialogue box. Go down to the **Save as type** and select the appropriate format.

**Note:** *When you do this you might lose some of the advanced formats or features of the current document.*

Most word processors will save in the usual Microsoft Word format with the .doc extension. They usually restrict this to the Word 6.0/95 format.

*HINT* If you want to save text for use in any word processor or DTP program, save it as Rich Text Format (.rtf). You might lose some advanced features but at least you can use it anywhere.

## Self-assessment questions

Consider the following self-assessment questions. These questions are intended to help you think through what you have learned in this chapter. Can you:

1. change text, colour, font and style?
2. insert an image on a page, alter the wrap format of the picture to be able to place it anywhere on a page?
3. insert a table into a document, make changes to the table using merge cells, borders and shading?
4. spell check and word count a document?
5. insert headers and footers into a document, including page numbers?

# 2 | Spreadsheets

## Introduction

Spreadsheets form a part of the professional use of ICT for many teachers. They are very useful in managing large amounts of data, automating calculations and speeding analysis. Mostly the data you will handle, as a teacher, will be associated with attainment. Using a spreadsheet will help you monitor changes over time, use comparative information, and develop target setting at individual, class and school levels.

Using performance data also enables you to track the effect of changes made to teaching, organisation, etc. that have been put in place to impact on standards. You are therefore able to provide evidence, very quickly, to reflect on the value of any changes that have been made.

Using a spreadsheet enables you to produce graphical information rapidly, and of high quality, for governors, senior management, etc.

Remember that producing, managing and analysing data does presume that you know what you are doing. Spreadsheets do not produce reliable results unless you have the right statistical understanding to know what you are requiring of the spreadsheet. *Passing the Numeracy Skills Test* in this series gives a good background in the section entitled 'Handling and Using Statistical Information'.

Although not impossible it would, in fact, be difficult for you to undertake the tasks in the ICT test without having practical experience of using a spreadsheet. You will most probably have a good working knowledge of word processing but will have had very little time to develop expertise in the use of spreadsheets. This section outlines the major skills and understanding of spreadsheets you will require for the test, plus a few others which will help you when setting up a spreadsheet with which to practise. It is worth sitting down with a computer and practising each of them, so that you feel secure in setting up a spreadsheet and using its facilities and functions. The test will not require you to set up a spreadsheet from scratch but will require you to be able to use the basic tools to edit, format and analyse data in an existing one.

The obvious choice for a spreadsheet is Excel. Although the features outlined in the next section are available on almost all spreadsheets, Excel is universally available and commonly used in schools.

However, all the Office suites I mention in the Introduction contain a spreadsheet. Indeed the level of skill required for the test is basic enough to be covered by spreadsheets designed for use by pupils in school.

In the introduction to Databases I mention the fact that both spreadsheets and databases now have similar functionality, which blurs the distinction somewhat. However, in the main, you are more likely to use the facilities of spreadsheet to support your professional work. The school will hold large administrative databases, which you might occasionally need to access.

Another factor to consider is the ease with which data can be transferred from database to spreadsheet. This means that the advanced statistical, charting and mathematical features of the spreadsheet can be combined with the ease of data management of the database.

# Spreadsheet basics

**Cell addressing**. A spreadsheet is basically a collection of individual cells as shown below. Each cell has a unique address given by its column and row.

|   | A | B | C | D | E | F | G |
|---|---|---|---|---|---|---|---|
| 1 |   |   |   |   |   |   |   |
| 2 |   |   |   |   |   |   |   |
| 3 |   |   |   |   |   |   |   |
| 4 |   |   |   |   |   |   |   |
| 5 |   |   |   |   |   |   |   |
| 6 |   |   |   |   |   |   |   |

Two cells are selected. The first has the address **C3** and the second **E4**.

**Placing and formatting information in cells**. Each cell can contain three types of information:

- **text;**
- **numerical;**
- **formulae.**

Text is mostly used for row and column labels. All text can be formatted by font, colour and alignment. These functions are similar to those in word processing.

Cells containing numerical data can be formatted to control how numbers will be shown, the most common will be:

- **to make them appear as currency or percentages;**
- **to control the number of decimal places shown.**

When formatting for decimal places, the computer will round your data to fit the number of decimal places you have chosen.

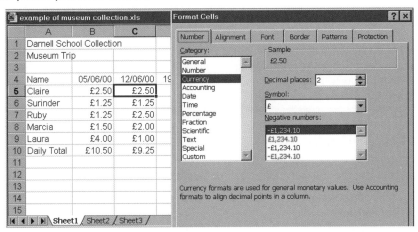

In the example above, cell C5 is being formatted to show currency to two decimal places.

The choices given in the test will be much simpler than those shown in the dialogue box above.

You can format a single cell or, by selecting a series of cells, you can format a number of cells at the same time.

**Make sure you can format cells for both text and number.**

Note: *When formatting cells to show percentage the spreadsheet automatically multiplies by 100 and puts in the % sign. If you had formatted a range of cells to show percentage and placed 0.75 into a cell it would show as 75%, but if you placed 75 into the cell it would appear as 7500%.*

**Changing the look of the spreadsheet.** Cells and groups of cells can be formatted to have a border, colour and shade fills, etc. This helps when you are laying out the spreadsheet. For example, you might want cells which show data in a specific colour to draw attention to them. You can also import graphics into a spreadsheet to enhance the look or to provide explanation for some of the data. These options can all be found in the **Format/Cells** menu.

**Using formulae and operators.** Formulae are mathematical expressions that allow you to take information from one or more cells and place the result of the calculation into another cell.

They are usually entered using a '=' sign in front of the formula. You will need to be able to use some of the more common formulae available to you. Many of these are entered by selecting the appropriate icon from the tools available at the top of the spreadsheet.

| | A | B | C | D | E | F | G |
|---|---|---|---|---|---|---|---|
| 1 | | Monday | Tuesday | Wednesday | Thursday | Friday | |
| 2 | Stock | 180 | =B4 | =C4 | | | |
| 3 | Sale | 54 | | | | | |
| 4 | | =B2−B3 | =C2−C3 | etc. | | | |
| 5 | | | | | | | |
| 6 | | | | | | | |

In the example above, a simple stock control spreadsheet is being developed. Cell B4 contains the formula B2−B3. This is a formula because it starts with the '=' sign.

However, when you look at the spreadsheet you will not see the formula in the cell, only the result. If you need to see the formula you placed in a cell, you need to return to the cell and click inside it to select it. You will then see the formula in the formula bar at the top of the spreadsheet just below the tool bar.

In this case the result of the formula =B2−B3 is 126. This result is then automatically transferred to cell C2 using the formula =B4. Then the process is repeated.

Spreadsheets use the following signs as mathematical operators

  *     for multiplication
  /     for division
  +     for addition
  −     for subtraction

**Note:** *It is very important to remember that a spreadsheet evaluates a formula using the order of operator precedence shown above. This means that 3+4\*5 produces the result 23 not 35. If the expression is written (3+4)\*5 the result would be 35 (because the spreadsheet works out the calculation in the bracket first).*

Check you can work out the results of the following calculations.

10\*5+(7−6)
(4\*5)−(8/2)
((5+5)−2)/2    The spreadsheet will evaluate the brackets from the inside out and then implement the division.

|   | A | B | C | D | E | F |
|---|---|---|---|---|---|---|
| 1 |  | Collection for museum trip |  |  |  |  |
| 2 | Name | 05/06/00 | 12/06/00 | 19/06/00 | 26/06/00 | Ind. Total |
| 3 | Laura | £2.50 | £1.25 | £0.00 | £1.25 | £5.00 |
| 4 | Daniel | £2.50 | £2.50 | £0.00 | £0.00 | £5.00 |
| 5 | Sharma | £1.25 | £1.25 | £2.50 | £0.00 | £5.00 |
| 6 | Darvinder | £1.25 | £2.50 | £0.00 | £1.25 | £5.00 |
| 7 | Claire | £2.50 | £0.00 | £2.50 | £0.00 | £5.00 |
| 8 | Daily Total | £10.00 | £7.50 | **=SUM(D3:D7)** | £2.50 |  |

In the example above, the formula in cell D8 creates the sum of the cells in the range D3:D7. All cell ranges are separated by a colon.

**Note:** *The columns A, D and F are wider than the other columns. All columns can be adjusted by dragging on the right hand boundary line of the column, in the column heading row, to help fit the data in the cells. Check you know how to do this.*

|   | A | B | C | D | E | F |
|---|---|---|---|---|---|---|
| 1 |  | Collection for museum trip |  |  |  |  |
| 2 | Name | 05/06/00 | 12/06/00 | 19/06/00 | 26/06/00 | Ind. Total |
| 3 | Laura | £2.50 | £1.25 | £0.00 | £1.25 | =SUM(B3:E3) |
| 4 | Daniel | £2.50 | £2.50 | £0.00 | £0.00 |  |
| 5 | Sharma | £1.25 | £1.25 | £2.50 | £0.00 |  |
| 6 | Darvinder | £1.25 | £2.50 | £0.00 | £1.25 |  |
| 7 | Claire | £2.50 | £0.00 | £2.50 | £0.00 |  |
| 8 | Daily Total | £10.00 | £7.50 | **=SUM(D3:D7)** | £2.50 |  |

When a formula is required in a series of cells such as F3 to F7 that gives the total for each row, as in the example above, you only need to:

1. enter the formula in the first cell, i.e. F3;
2. select the cell by left clicking in it;
3. copy the contents using **Edit/Copy** or selecting the **copy icon**;
4. select the range of cells in which you want to place the formula, by clicking in the first cell of the range and dragging down until all the cells you want are selected;
5. then paste in the formula using **Edit/Paste** or the **paste icon**.

The spreadsheet will automatically adjust the cell references.

At first this seems a long way round but with practice it will become a very useful tool. It really speeds up spreadsheet development.

**Try this several times to ensure you know how it works. It is easy to make mistakes.**

The tool bar in the example above shows two icons that help automate the entry of formulae. The first is the Σ symbol. Clicking on the cell where you want your formula and selecting the Σ icon will automatically insert a formula to calculate the sum. It also checks for a range of numerical data either in the same column above or in the same row to the left and selects this as well. Be careful, as this selection might not contain the data you require. Always check the range of data selected automatically. **Ensure you can use this automated feature.**

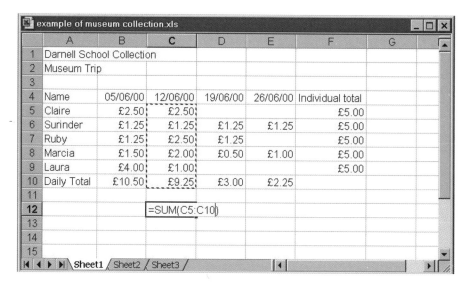

If you are not happy with the range of data selected by the computer then all you need do is delete the value in the brackets, go to the start of your data and left click, drag down to select the whole range and the addresses will be inserted in the formula for you. This is shown above.

It is more than likely that you will require a number of other functions in your use of spreadsheets. This is particularly true if you use a spreadsheet to track achievement.

The three main functions you will require are **average, median** and **frequency**. These are accessed in Excel by clicking the icon with the $fx$ symbol, then going to the statistical operators and choosing average or median.

There are a lot of functions to choose from, more than you will normally need.

It is likely that the test might ask you to insert a simple formula to calculate the sum, average or median of a group of data (e.g. in a column or row). However, this will be a simple choice from the menu and you will have a very limited range of functions to choose from, so don't panic when you see the choices available in spreadsheets such as Excel.

**Note:** *Once again the automated features make entering the formulae very easy but also liable to error. Ensure that the data range is properly selected. The spreadsheet will ignore spaces contained in the data range.*

For more information on the frequency function see the end of this chapter.

**Sorting data**. You will often need to sort tables of data into different orders, e.g. by name, gender, class, year group, etc.

The ability to do this is built into all spreadsheets and accessed in Excel through **Data – Sort**. You can sort data in ascending or descending values, and the sort will work on several fields, e.g. by surname and then by forename.

**Note:** *You must select the data you wish to sort before you trigger the sort function. If you have a spreadsheet such as in the last example and select the column data containing the names of the children (A5:A9) then you can sort this by descending or ascending alphabetical order. However, be careful as the rest of the data will not move with the sorted names and thus the link between the money paid and the names will be lost. You must select all data that is associated together, before you sort a particular column; this way the data will follow the new, sorted, order. Most spreadsheets should warn you of this.*

**Presenting information in a chart**. The graph function in spreadsheets is one of the most automated. However, it needs watching carefully as it makes assumptions about what you want. Although a spreadsheet will draw a graph of any data you select, it is better to ensure that the data has a label and the label is included in the selection. The computer can distinguish between text and numerical data and will automatically include the label in the chart.

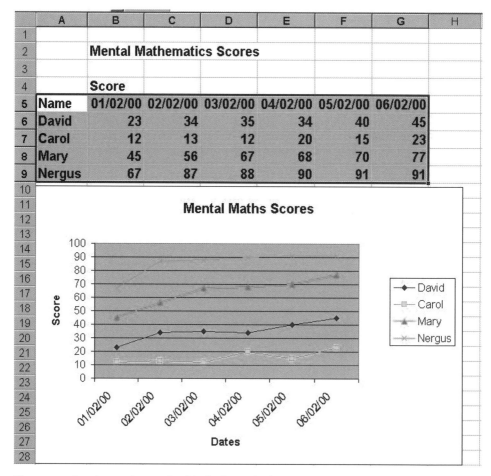

| | A | B | C | D | E | F | G | H |
|---|---|---|---|---|---|---|---|---|
| 1 | | | | | | | | |
| 2 | | Mental Mathematics Scores | | | | | | |
| 3 | | | | | | | | |
| 4 | | Score | | | | | | |
| 5 | Name | 01/02/00 | 02/02/00 | 03/02/00 | 04/02/00 | 05/02/00 | 06/02/00 | |
| 6 | David | 23 | 34 | 35 | 34 | 40 | 45 | |
| 7 | Carol | 12 | 13 | 12 | 20 | 15 | 23 | |
| 8 | Mary | 45 | 56 | 67 | 68 | 70 | 77 | |
| 9 | Nergus | 67 | 87 | 88 | 90 | 91 | 91 | |

The example above shows the kind of graph that was produced by selecting the data shown and then using the automated functions.

The type of graph chosen to represent this data was a **line graph**.

**Note:** *Make sure you know the appropriate use of each type of graph.*

**Bar chart**
*This is used to show the relative sizes of sets of data. The graph for frequency distribution of reading ages would be a bar chart giving a graphical representation of the comparative numbers or percentage of children falling into each interval.*

**Line graph**
*This is used to show how data is changing. Usually this is change over time, as shown in the example above.*

**Pie chart**
*This is used to show the proportion of the whole formed by individual data. An example of this might be the ethnic composition of a school population or the split of children travelling to school by a variety of means.*

### Scatter graph

*This is used to plot two quantities that are possibly related. The scatter graph will show the degree of this relationship. For instance, you might plot the English SAT scores and Standard Reading Scores to look at the range of reading scores that relate to a particular SAT level, giving some means of using the reading scores as a predictor of eventual SAT achievement. Another use might be to plot percentage attendance against SAT achievement to see if there is a relationship.*

The data used above was in rows. You might need to use the data series from the columns – make sure you can make this change in the chart wizard. There is usually a choice of row or column for the series of data from the selection you have made in the spreadsheet. For example, you might need to plot the scores of individual children for one particular date.

It is possible to plot selected groups of data from within the chart wizard. For example, you might wish to plot the change in scores for two individual children whose data is not contiguous, e.g. David and Mary in the example above. To do this in Excel you use the **series tab** from the chart wizard. Then select each child's data as a separate series. Currently the test does not ask you to make a graph from spreadsheet data. However, it has in the past and this is a 'must-have' skill for your work in schools.

**Inserting rows and columns**. However clever you are, you might forget to include a column or row of data. Worry not! The designers of spreadsheet software have included the handy tool of inserting a row or column, and the clever bit is that as the rows or columns move apart all the formulae are automatically adjusted to take account of the change.

To do this, first select the column or row by clicking in the header, e.g. 'A' for column A or '5' for row 5. Then go to menu option **Insert/Row** or **Insert/Column**. Rows are inserted above the selected row and columns to the left of the selected column.

**Databases and spreadsheets**. Data can be moved between applications and this allows you to use the different functions of each application to best effect. In the chapter on databases there is the start of an assessment database. Below is the same database exported to Excel as a spreadsheet (with the .xls file extension).

| | A | B | C | D | E | F | G | H | I |
|---|---|---|---|---|---|---|---|---|---|
| 1 | ID | First Name | Second Name | Age | Date of Birth | Meals | English SAT level | Maths SAT level | Science SAT level |
| 2 | 1 | Joe | Soap | 11 | 22/08/89 | sandwiches | 0 | 0 | 0 |
| 3 | 2 | Claire | Soap | 8 | 23/04/92 | sandwiches | 0 | 0 | 0 |
| 4 | 3 | Fred | Bloggs | 3 | 23/08/97 | free | 0 | 0 | 0 |
| 5 | 4 | Mary | Bloggs | 4 | 23/05/96 | free | 0 | 0 | 0 |
| 6 | 5 | Charles | Doe | 9 | 02/04/91 | paid | 0 | 0 | 0 |
| 7 | 6 | Margaret | Flower | 9 | 05/06/91 | free | 0 | 0 | 0 |

You can see that this is the same as the table layout in Access. Note that the column headings are the fields and the rows labels are the records.

If you wanted to add a field in Excel then you will need to insert a column or use the next available column and type the field name into the first cell of the column. Any data in that column is assumed to belong to that field, so ensure that the data is formatted correctly, i.e. by selecting the number of cells in the column you are going to use and then going to **Format/Cells** and selecting the appropriate formatting option from the dialogue box.

When you move data between a database and a spreadsheet application the most reliable method is to export the data in a form that the other program can read.

However, the data below was inserted into a Word document by selecting the data required in the Access table, copying this and then pasting it into the Word document. It appears in the Word document as a table. The same can be done in Excel where the data will paste into an Excel worksheet.

| ID | First Name | Second Name | Age | Date of Birth | Meals | English SAT level | Maths SAT level | Science SAT level |
|----|-----------|-------------|-----|---------------|-------|-------------------|-----------------|-------------------|
| 1 | Joe | Soap | 11 | 22/08/89 | sandwiches | 0 | 0 | 0 |
| 2 | Claire | Soap | 8 | 23/04/92 | sandwiches | 0 | 0 | 0 |
| 3 | Fred | Bloggs | 3 | 23/08/97 | free | 0 | 0 | 0 |
| 4 | Mary | Bloggs | 4 | 23/05/96 | free | 0 | 0 | 0 |
| 5 | Charles | Doe | 9 | 02/04/91 | paid | 0 | 0 | 0 |
| 6 | Margaret | Flower | 9 | 05/06/91 | free | 0 | 0 | 0 |

This is a very useful technique for getting data from one application to another, i.e. for a report; but not a good idea for large or complex data.

Although spreadsheets seem to have so many complex functions and tools, they are, at heart, a simple way of managing and manipulating data. People seldom use more than a fraction of the potential available and the test will use only simple generic functions and operations. So set up a few spreadsheets and have a go.

For the more adventurous a few extra notes follow below.

# Not in the test but useful to know

The **frequency** function is very useful in preparing data for graphs to show distribution of scores, e.g. standardised reading test scores. Frequency of data is usually grouped together in intervals (see *Numeracy Skills Test*, page 31).

These intervals are known as **bin values** in the frequency function. This can be a bit confusing but in reality is quite easy.

| | A | B | C | D | E | F | G |
|----|-----|-----|-----|-----|-----|-----|-----|
| 1 | | **Reading test scores** | | | **Bin values** | | |
| 2 | | | | | | | |
| 3 | Robin | 112 | | | 70 | | |
| 4 | Clare | 105 | | | 85 | | |
| 5 | Bertram | 89 | | | 115 | | |
| 6 | John | 78 | | | 130 | | |
| 7 | Megan | 102 | | | | | |
| 8 | Susie | 87 | | | | | |
| 9 | David | 70 | | | | | |
| 10 | | | | | | | |

In the example above it has been decided that the data will be placed in the following intervals:

0–70
71–85
86–115
116–130
>130

The bin values shown will give these intervals. The computer will place the number of scores falling in the range 0–70 in **F3**, scores falling in the range 71–85 in **F4,** and so on. Note that you need to select one more cell than your bin values for values greater than the last bin value. However, you could also set the maximum bin value you expect.

**Note:** *You will need to practise using this function. In Excel it appears by clicking on the fχ symbol and also under* **Tools – Data Analysis – Histogram.** *This is an* **add-in** *called Analysis ToolPack and needs to be installed from the CD if you cannot find it in* **Tools – Data Analysis – Histogram.**

**Absolute cell reference**. When the cell references change as the formula is copied, these are called relative references. Occasionally you might not want one of the cell references to change.

For instance, you might have a spreadsheet of the sale of school sweatshirts of different sizes that calculates the profit against a fixed percentage. The school might lower or raise this percentage depending on sales over the year. This percentage needs to be put into a single cell that is used by series of formulae and which must not change. This is called absolute referencing.

| | A | B | C | D | E | F | G |
|---|---|---|---|---|---|---|---|
| 1 | | A | B | C | Percentage profit | | 10% |
| 2 | Size | Sales | Wholesale price | Retail price | Total | | |
| 3 | 5 to 7 | 45 | £3.00 | =C3+ ((C3/100)*$G$1) | £148.50 | | |
| 4 | 7 to 9 | 24 | £3.50 | £3.85 | £84.00 | | |
| 5 | 9 to 11 | 56 | £4.00 | £4.40 | £224.00 | | |
| 6 | Adult | 20 | £5.00 | £5.50 | £110.00 | | |

The formula in D3 is an example of the one used in the cell range D3:D6. Putting this into D3 and then copying it down the column will result in the wholesale price cell references changing from C3 through to C6. However, the cell G1 contains the fixed profit percentage decided by the school. This must not change and so the cell reference is $G$1. Putting the $ sign before the column and row makes the cell reference absolute.

## Self-assessment questions

Consider the following self-assessment questions. These questions are intended to help you think through what you have learned in this chapter. Can you:

1. format a cell for number (currency, percentage, etc.) fill and border?
2. insert a formula into a cell, e.g. to add the contents of a selected cell range?
3. create a graph from selected cell data?
4. copy a graph into another type of document, e.g. PowerPoint?
5. use an absolute cell reference?

# 3 | Databases

## Introduction

In the past, the ICT skills test has included the use of a database application. This has been dropped from the current test. However, the tests change each year and as the use of a database application is an important component in ICT skill development, you will still find it valuable to look through this section. Many people find databases a little difficult to understand. Mostly this is because they are usually only found in an administrative role and, unlike word processing, email and spreadsheets, not often used at home.

It is well worth learning how to create and use a database, as it is a very efficient way of handling certain kinds of data. There are really two common forms of database – the **flat file** and the **relational**. While the most common databases are relational, e.g. Microsoft Access, Filemaker Pro, etc., these are really 'industrial strength' programs and provide facilities and power that only an organisation would require. Teachers would rarely need anything more powerful than a 'flat file' database and it is interesting to note that database programs written for use by children such as Information Workshop and Junior ViewPoint can often provide all the facilities you will need.

What is the difference between a flat file and a relational database?

The **flat file** is so called because it resembles the traditional card index system. Imagine a drawer in your local library that contains cards about all the books on the shelves. The drawer is marked 'fiction' and this is the name of the database. Each card in that drawer represents a record and the data or information on each card is organised into **'fields'**, e.g.

> Author;
> Publisher;
> Illustrator;
> ISBN;
> Date of Purchase.

A flat file computer database reproduces this system inside the computer and provides you with tools to search, order and manipulate the data in a way that would be very difficult with the old card index.

The **relational** database does all that the flat file one does, but it has the ability to link tables of data together. This is a common feature of schools' administrative databases. The children form the main link between tables but each table might hold different kinds of data about the children.

| Personal Information | Home Information | School Information | Assessment Information | Medical Information |
|---|---|---|---|---|

For example, each of these tables has common fields such as the admission number of the pupil and the pupil's name. However, the Home Information table will contain fields such as address, emergency contacts, etc., the Personal Information table might contain parents' names, date of birth, religion, home language, etc.

A relational database is able to use all the links between the data and produce reports, forms, etc. based on these relationships. For example, a report might contain information from several different tables. Working this way means that data with common properties can be held in individual, but linked, tables; to replicate this in a flat file system would mean using different databases, with no linkage between them.

In this chapter you will find some additional skills that will allow you to use a database for your own professional use. It is worth setting up a simple database and learning how it is designed, the various types of field and how the data can be queried.

The first problem you will encounter in using a database is the fundamental one of 'do I need to use a database for this?' Over the last few years spreadsheets have come to have many of the features of a database. In Excel you can create fields, search for specific data and do many other things that were traditionally the preserve of the database. It is often more appropriate to use a spreadsheet for managing data which you wish to present graphically or analyse statistically, e.g. assessment data.

You would choose to use a database to manage data, where you have the need to produce fairly complex reports or where you need to do sophisticated searches. A search that uses multiple criteria is often easier using a database, e.g. the SAT scores for all girls on free meals in Classes 5, 6 and 7. You can do some statistical analysis using a database, e.g. giving the average SAT score for the pupils in the above query.

**Note:** *All personal data held on a computer must conform to the requirements of the Data Protection Act. All schools have registered a range of fields of data they are likely to use. Please check that any data you plan to use is covered by your school's registration.*

# Database basic skills

**Designing a database**. You need to be clear from the start as to the purpose of the database. This way you will know what fields you are likely to require and what type they will be (see later).

For example, if you wished to explore the various factors that might affect attainment then leaving out 'meals' as a field takes away your ability to look for the possible relationship between 'free meals' and attainment.

> *HINT*  Planning also helps you decide on which are unnecessary fields, e.g. it is not really relevant to have a pupil's home address in a database used to explore issues around attainment.

**Creating a database**. Databases require you to give a name to your file immediately, so that the program can lay down the structure in the file as you develop the database.

Usually there is some helpful mechanism to guide you through the creation process. Microsoft's Access gives you the choice of some pre-built databases to choose from. If these do not suit your needs then you can create your own, in which case you will be taken to the table section and presented with a blank table like the one on page 34:

| Field Name | Data Type | Description |
|---|---|---|
| First Name | Text | |
| Last Name | Text | |
| Age | Number | |
| Date of Birth | Date/Time | |
| ▶ Meals | Text ▼ | |
| | Text | |
| | Memo | |
| | Number | |
| | Date/Time | |
| | Currency | |
| | AutoNumber | |
| | Yes/No | |
| | OLE Object | |
| | Hyperlink | |
| | Lookup Wizard... | |

Here four fields have already been entered and the fifth is now being set up. You will see that the fields have different types of data associated with them, e.g. text, number, yes/no, etc. It is important to get the choice right, otherwise you might find difficulty later on. In the case of the 'Meals' field it would be best to use the **Lookup Wizard** and give a range of fixed choices for the field, e.g. free, paid, sandwiches, home. This helps to prevent typing errors when entering data, as the user just selects from a drop down choice menu. (See the later section on data entry forms.)

> HINT    Make sure you are careful with the type of field. As you can see there are special ones for date and currency. The date type is very important as it allows you to do specific things with the date information that would be difficult if you entered the date as a text field, e.g. find all DoB between 01/09/89 and 31/12/89.

You need to practise setting up several databases to get the hang of all this. There are, of course, a whole range of other things you can do to a field such as prevent data outside a certain range being entered. If you need to do something special then that is the time to learn how to do it – for the present we will stick to simple basic skills.

You can add, delete or edit a field any time you like by going to this table (in design view or editing view) and either removing the field (which will remove any associated data), editing the type of field or field name, or adding a new field.

**Note:** *If a field is numerical then you can control the appearance of the data in the same way as you can for a spreadsheet, e.g. how many decimal places, etc.*

Another feature of the fields is the size. You can specify how large you wish the field to be. If you do not do this then the program will use default values, which might not always suit your purpose. This is particularly true of names, which can be quite short in this country but can be significantly longer for some children coming from other countries.

**Creating a data entry form.** To make life easier all databases allow you to create a data entry form that you can layout in any way you wish and which makes the entry of the information easier for the person who has to do it. You can do this with a 'wizard' or by yourself.

Here is an example:

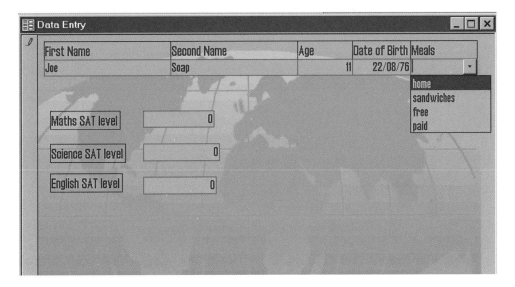

Note the drop-down menu for the **Meals** field. You can see that this form would make data entry much easier.

On a form like this it is easier for the user to move between fields using the **Tab** key. You can set something called the **Tab Order** for the fields in the form. This allows you to guide the data entry as the user presses the **Tab** key. In Access this is achieved by right clicking inside the form and selecting the **Tab Order** option. You can then select the order from the dialogue box.

You can use forms for a whole range of operations including setting up queries.

**Finding information.** The simplest way is to use the **Find** option in the **Edit** menu. This is a very simple search tool and will either search the whole database or a selected field. It will also allow you to search for a complete or partial match. You will need to experiment with this to find data. It is quick and easy and will, for example, allow you to find a name even if you cannot remember the full spelling.

This is done by using a simple, or more complex, query to search the database. The idea of the query is that it allows you to set up the criteria for the data you are searching for, e.g. you might want to find all the children who are older than 8 years of age, in which case your query would be based on the **Age** field and would be **Age > 8**.

Look at how this is achieved in Access:

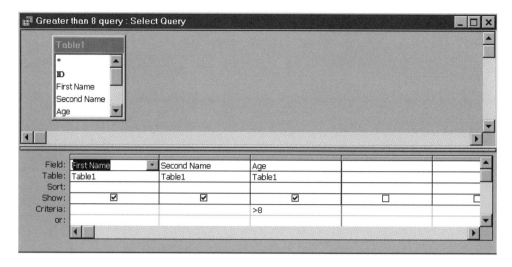

This query will show information in the following fields when it is used:

**First Name    Second Name    Age**

Under the field **Age** the **Criteria** has been set to **>8**. This query is then saved with an appropriate name and when used again it will find all the children whose age is greater than 8 and show the data in the above fields for each child.

You could also add other criteria for other fields, e.g. **Age >8 and Meals = "Free"**. Notice the use of 'and'. Using these two criteria together means that the database has to find data matching the first criteria and data matching the second criteria. It will reject all other data. In some databases you can type this query in as a sentence and the database will then process the data.

Although there is a common set of operators which databases recognise, there are variations in how the database allows you to set up a query.

Here are some of the more common query syntax terms which you will need to know:

> **x**            means find all values greater than the value *x*;
< **x**            means find all values less than the value *x*;
> = **x**         means find all values greater than or equal to the value *x*;
< = **x**         means find all values less than or equal to the value *x*.

These operators can also be used with text fields or date fields.

> = **"Bloggs"**        This will find all names equal to Bloggs and any other names
                        between Bloggs and the end of the alphabet.

The name Bloggs is in inverted commas to show that it is text.

**Between 10 and 20** This will find all data in the field between these two values.

Sometimes you do not know the whole spelling of an item of data, e.g. street name or surname. Maybe you only know three or four letters. The database allows you to make a query that looks for these letters within a text field. Sometimes it uses the syntax contains or includes.

For example, **contains "har"** will find all references to Harry, hare, Harold, hardy, charity, share, etc. Sometimes you can use **begins with "har"** which will only find words using these three letters at the start.

Access lets you put in a wild card (using the * character) to find particular parts of text. It also uses the syntax **Like** to search for groups of characters.

For example, **"har*"** will find Harry, hare, Harold, hardy; **"*har*"** will find charity, share.

Look at this example:

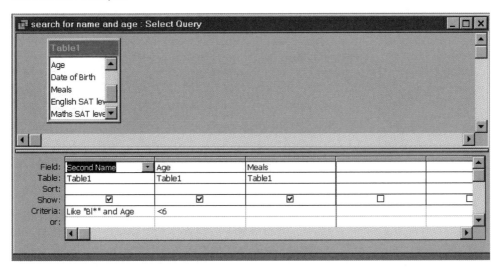

Here the search criteria has two parts. Firstly we want to find any child whose surname begins with **Bl and** then we only want those children whose age is **less than 6**. Notice once again the 'and'. If the criteria in an Access query are on the same line for different fields then the search has an **and** condition.

Written as a sentence it would look like this;

**Second Name Like "Bl*" and Age <6**

The result of this query is a set of records that match the criteria.

Note that the computer was asked to give information in the Meals field for the records that matched the criteria.

This set of data is part of the whole database but once you have run the query you will be working with this subset until you request all the records again.

AND, OR and NOT are very useful and are called Boolean operators. However, it is very easy to make mistakes with them and create queries that the computer cannot run.

We have seen the use of the **and** operator. The **or** operator does what you would expect, it will 'find this match or that match'.

For example, **Second Name Like "Bl*" or Age >6**

| search for name or age : Selec... _ □ × | |
|---|---|
| **Second Name** | **Age** |
| ▶ Flower | 9 |
| Soap | 8 |
| Bloggs | 3 |
| Bloggs | 4 |
| Doe | 9 |
| Soap | 11 |
| * | 0 |

Record: ◄◄ ◄ 1 ► ►► ►* of 6

Here the computer will find all children with the Second Name which starts with Bl and it will also find all the children who are over the age of six.

The Boolean operator **not** is also quite useful. This is used to exclude records on a match.

For example, **Not Second Name Like "Bl*"** would exclude all children with names beginning with Bl.

**Sorting a field**. Any field can be sorted in either ascending or descending order. Indeed you can select two fields and the database will sort on the first fields and then the second, e.g. select First Name and Second Name and the database will give both in alphabetical order.

**Note:** *Unlike a spreadsheet, if you select one field and sort this in ascending order, all other fields and data will also be re-ordered in the database as the program knows they are related.*

Although there is a great deal to learn about databases in general, the above should cover more than you will need for the test.

## *Self-assessment questions*

Consider the following self-assessment questions. These questions are intended to help you think through what you have learned in this chapter. Can you:

1. set up a database using appropriate field types?
2. create a data entry form?
3. use the simple find tool?
4. construct a more complex query to search a database?
5. sort a database using one field?

# 4 | E-mail

## Introduction

The e-mail application has become one of the most useful and popular of the Internet. In fact electronic mailing systems have been around for a very long time and indeed go back to the early days of the Internet.

Obviously for the majority of personal users e-mail is a quick, convenient and easy way to keep in contact. However, it has offered possibilities in the field of education, which have yet to reach their full potential. Teachers can communicate rapidly with each other, sharing ideas, documents (e.g. lesson plans, resources such as texts for the Literacy Hour, Schemes of Work) and images.

If this applies to teachers imagine the impact it has on pupils. The power to be able to communicate with children across the world brings a whole new perspective to the learning environment. There are many opportunities within the subject curricula to take advantage of the communication offered by e-mail.

The inclusion of the use of e-mail in the test shows that it is a tool that is seen to be of growing importance. Peculiarly it is the one with which most students are familiar.

Once again the caveat 'Don't be over confident' is still worth heeding. Go through this chapter and make sure you know how to perform all the skills outlined.

You will use e-mail in three main forms. The first is the more common POP3 account (this stands for Post Office Protocol, third attempt) and the second is the older SMTP (Simple Mail Transport Protocol). Some e-mail programs use SMTP to send mail and POP3 to receive mail. Luckily you do not have to worry about how these work. If you have to set up an e-mail program, your Internet Service Provider will give you details of the mail servers it uses and where to place the information to set up the e-mail program.

There are several common e-mail programs that use the above protocols, such as Outlook Express, Eudora and Thunderbird.

Outlook is now the most commonly used e-mail program and has a range of functionality which allows synchronisation with some smart phones, excellent calendar management etc. It is worth learning to use as you can set up a series of filters for your e-mails which gives you greater control over your e-mail management.

Another form of e-mail is now becoming more common. The problem of using programs such as Express is that you either need to take your computer with you, if you are on the move (i.e. a Laptop), or you need to borrow one and configure it to talk to your Internet Service Providers in order to download your mail.

The way around this is to use Web Mail. This works over the World Wide Web and can be accessed anywhere in the world by a computer connected to the Internet and having a browser such as Internet Explorer or Firefox. The most common version of this is Hotmail from Microsoft; there are many others on the net. Internet Service Providers use POP3, etc. but also allow access to the account from the web.

Backpackers everywhere have discovered the value of being able to send and receive mail anywhere in the connected world. Indeed it appears that there are few countries in which it is impossible to pay for a short period on a computer in order to contact friends and parents, etc.

# E-mail basics

The test will use the most common generic features of e-mail. As with all the other applications in the tests, it is menu driven rather than including an icon tool bar.

**E-mail addresses**. These are instantly recognisable because of the @ character in the middle, e.g.:

tony@innotts.co.uk

The account is for someone called Tony and the mail server is provided by the ISP innotts. The mail server is called mail.innotts.co.uk. This server takes Tony's outgoing mail and sends it to the recipient based on the address given in the header of the e-mail. It also stores incoming e-mail and sends it on to Tony when he logs on.

Web Mail addresses have the same format, e.g.

tony@hotmail.com

The use of lower case is most common and the addresses are usually case sensitive.

**Sending a new e-mail**. Here is the 'compose new message' screen from Outlook Express, found in the menu under **Message/New Message**:

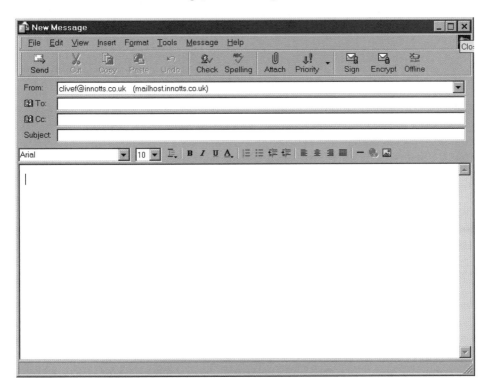

The program automatically inserts your address in the **'From'** box. You can then insert the address of the person to whom you are sending the e-mail by typing it into the **'To'** box. If you want to send it more than one person you can type additional addresses in there, separated by a **semicolon ';'**.

There is another box titled 'Subject'. It is best to fill this in. All recipients of e-mail see a list that shows who the e-mail is from, its subject and date/time received. If you leave out the subject then this will be blank in the list and your e-mail might get ignored or left till later. Filling in the Subject option ensures that the recipient knows what the e-mail is about and is more likely to open it.

You only need to insert a short sentence or phrase in the Subject box, e.g. 'About the TDA skills test' then the recipient will know you have information or a query about the test.

The rest of the space in the New Message window is for the actual message. You will note that all the usual text format options are available, including a simple spell check.

**Sending a copy to someone else**. In the example above, you will see a box titled **'Cc'**. This allows you to send a copy of the e-mail to other interested people. As with the main address box, you can enter one address or many addresses. This is common for things such as the minutes of a meeting where the main e-mail will go to the Chair but all members receive a copy.

**Using the Address Book to manage contacts**. As you use e-mail more frequently you will build up a list of contacts. There is an easy way to manage this list called the Address Book. Most e-mail programs have this facility and it makes life much easier.

Look again at the **'To'** box and you will see a little book icon next to the **'To'** title. Click here and it will take you to the Address Book. You can then select addresses of the person/persons you want to receive the e-mail. At the same time you can add any contacts that need to receive a copy of the e-mail.

The other route to the Address Book is through the main menu under **Tools/Address Book** in Outlook Express and **View/Address Book** in the test.

**Adding, editing and deleting an Address**. How this is done varies from program to program. There will either be an option on the main menu to go to the Address Book (as mentioned above) and from here you can add a contact or edit existing ones, or there will be similar choices directly from the main menu (this is the format chosen for the test), where there is a menu option **Addresses** which will give you the option to add an address or delete one, etc.

**Finding an address in the Address Book**. The Address Book has a simple find function. In Outlook Express this is a button called 'Find People'. This function is not implemented in the test and you will simply scroll through a short list of addresses. However, for your own use you might need this to find a contact in a large Address Book. Contacts are usually listed by name so your search is for the name of the person.

**Finding an address of someone not in the Address Book**. This is a very useful function. You might have forgotten the address of a contact and wonder how you will make contact again. Fortunately there are things called Directory Services on the Internet, e.g. Yahoo!, People Search, Bigfoot Internet Directory Service, etc. When you select the Find People button in Outlook Express you can either search the local Address Book or go to the built-in Directory Services (you can add ones of your own as well). Provided you are connected to the Internet then the program will search the chosen Directory Service for the e-mail address of the person for whom you are searching.

**Sending an e-mail to groups of people with a common interest**. This is a valuable and time-saving concept. You can organise the contacts of your Address Book into groups. You can still find their individual addresses but they might also be part of a group such as Literacy Coordinators. The useful bit of this is that you can type the group name into the box titled '**To**' and the e-mail will be sent to all members of the group.

E-mail programs will vary in how they let you do this but there will be an option in the menu to create a **New Group** and attach contacts to this group.

**Organising your contacts**. You can also organise your contacts into folders for your own convenience, e.g. all friends in a folder called '**Personal**' and professional contacts in a folder called '**Work**'.

Another useful option in the Address Book is to be able to sort your contacts by name (ascending or descending), address or phone number.

**Adding a file to your e-mail**. These are called **attachments** and help to make e-mail such a valuable tool for communication. Any file, e.g. documents, spreadsheets, images, etc., can be sent via e-mail. Obviously they are only useful if the recipient has the correct program to open the files.

If you look at the example screen at the beginning of this chapter, you will see the menu option **Insert**. Under this is the option for **File Attachment**. If you select File  Attachment you will be taken to a dialogue box that requests the location and name of the file. It will allow you to browse for these. Once you have selected the file the name will appear in a new box titled '**Attach**'. This will also give the type of file and its size.

Note:     *There is a limit to the size of files that can be sent with an e-mail. All e-mails are stored on the ISP's mail server and take up space until they are downloaded. The rules vary between ISPs but a guide figure would be about 10 Mb as the maximum file size.*

It is worth knowing that the **Insert** menu option also allows you to insert text or a picture into your actual e-mail. The problem here is that not all e-mail programs will be able to display pictures, so you need to know whether your recipient has an older text-only mail program or one that can display pictures.

**Saving a part-finished e-mail**. When you are creating an e-mail you might not have time to finish it and need to come back to it later before you actually send it. To do this you just go to the File/Save menu option and save it. It will go in a special folder, e.g. Draft in Outlook Express. You can retrieve it from here later on by selecting the folder and then your e-mail.

**Sending your e-mail**. When you have finished creating your e-mail in the message window then all you have to do is just click the **Send** button or go to the menu **File/Send message** option. It will then be placed in the **Outbox folder**. From here it is automatically sent whilst you are connected or will be sent next time you log on.

**Receiving an e-mail**. You will usually receive your e-mails when you log on to your Internet Service Provider and start your e-mail program, or you start your browser and go to your Web Mail provider.

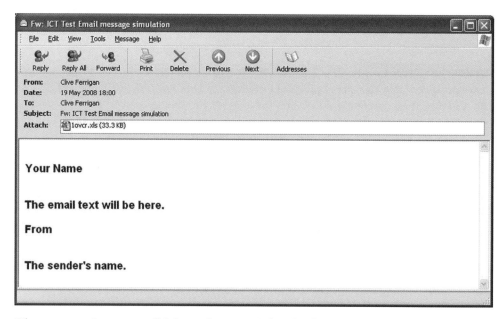

When you receive an e-mail it is put into your **Inbox** by the program. Clicking on the Inbox folder will then show you all your current e-mails. Most e-mail programs automatically open in the inbox folder and show you its contents.

The program also differentiates between 'read' and 'unread' e-mails, usually by showing unread ones in bold type.

The example above shows a received test e-mail as it appears in Outlook Express. Most e-mail programs provide a similar window for reading new e-mails.

**Managing your e-mails**. You can set up folders of your own and move e-mails to these folders. For example, you might be a member of an ICT coordinators group that exchanges information. Creating a folder named 'ICT Group' and moving these e-mails to this folder will allow you to find them more easily.

**Replying to an e-mail**. In the example above, you can see header information that shows who the e-mail was from, the subject and the address of the recipient.

You now have a quick way of replying to this e-mail, without having to go to the new message option and inserting addresses, etc. Just click on the **Reply** button or select the **Message/Reply** menu option.

When you select the reply option you get a similar window to the New Message window but the address box '**To**' is now filled in with the address of the sender. The original text of the message is left for you to refer to, edit or delete as you see fit. Sometimes people become lazy and reply to an e-mail leaving the original text, the recipient then replies back leaving two sets of original text, etc. This can generate quite a large e-mail if it continues.

**Forwarding a message**. If you think someone else might be interested in the e-mail just click the **Forward** button or choose **Message/Forward** from the menu and you will then be asked to give the address of the recipient. At this point you can either type in the address or use the Address Book.

*HINT* You also have the group option and if you forward to a group name then everyone in the group will receive the e-mail.

**Receiving an attachment**. You can see that there is an attachment with the e-mail in the example above. The attachment is a document file called spreadsheet.doc and is 535 KB in size.

You can do two things to this attachment. You can save it to disc by going to **File/Save Attachments** or you can open it directly by double clicking on it. The latter will only work if you have the appropriate program to read the file (in this case Microsoft Word).

Note: *Documents with the extension .doc, for example, might be created with different versions of Microsoft Word. Be careful to ensure that your recipient has the correct version of the program you are using to create a file, or save the file in the earliest convenient form of the program, e.g. Word 6. Microsoft Word 97 will not read Word 2000 documents but Word 2000 will read Word 97 documents; all will read Word 6. This applies to files from all programs where there are updated versions; they are usually upwardly compatible but not the reverse.*

**Guarding against viruses**. It is dangerous to open any attachment by double clicking it unless you are certain of the source and that the source uses a virus scanner.

Viruses can be spread by e-mail. They usually reside in an attachment, although there are security weaknesses in individual programs, which allow viruses to come in through other means. Be careful about opening an attachment from an unknown source.

Save it to file and then scan it before use. Any file attachment which ends in an '**.exe**' extension is an executable program file and will run as soon as you double click on it. By the time you find out that this really is a virus, the damage will be done. The problem is that if you are on a network it can spread throughout an institution. It can also send itself to your friends through your e-mails.

**Looking at a sent e-mail**. Received e-mails are usually opened by simply double clicking them and a new window opens showing the text of the e-mail.

## Self-assessment questions

Consider the following self-assessment questions. These questions are intended to help you think through what you have learned in this chapter. Can you:

1. compose an e-mail and send to a specific address?
2. set up an address book, add, delete and edit contacts?
3. create a group within the address book?
4. send an e-mail to a group?
5. add an attachment to an e-mail?
6. copy an e-mail to another recipient?

# 5 | The Internet

## Introduction

It is more than likely that you will already be an experienced user of the Internet and World Wide Web. Access to the largest information base in the world is becoming an important part of our lives. It is also the most amazing resource for children and teachers.

There is a difference between the Internet and the World Wide Web. The Internet has many functions and is basically a very large network, which links other networks and individuals. This allows users to do a variety of things including sending email and using the World Wide Web, which is just one of many tools that use the Internet to transport information.

When people talk of the Internet they often mean the World Wide Web (WWW for short). This is because the WWW is the most often used component of the Internet.

To access the WWW you need to use a program called a browser. The two main browsers are Microsoft's Internet Explorer and Mozilla Firefox. There are other browsers which provide the same facilities. For example, there are several which run with the Linux Operating System. However, the test will just use the basic generic functions of any browser.

Many people find the Internet useful but have difficulty getting information. They often end up with thousands of web pages after their search, and get frustrated with the whole thing. This is a shame because all that is required are some simple techniques to refine your search and get closer to the information you want.

The test will simulate a simple search for information from a specific web site. It is important to be able to do this for the test, but also for your own use.

## Basic Internet skills

This section outlines the basic functions of a browser and how to search more effectively.

**Web addresses**. We are familiar with the basic format of web addresses, e.g.:

**http://www.dfes.gov.uk**

This breaks down to:

http:   means Hypertext Transfer Protocol. This indicates that the files being transferred will be in HTML (Hypertext Markup Language) format. This is the language that makes your web pages appear on any computer in roughly the same format.

www.   means that this is using the World Wide Web.

dfes.   means go to the site which has the domain name 'dfes'. Domain names are the Internet's way of managing addresses. Your ISP will have its own domain name and your e-mail address might be bloggs@freeserve.co.uk where 'freeserve' is the domain name for the Internet Service Provider (ISP). All domain names must be registered and sometimes there is a charge. Many companies, schools and some individuals have their own domain names.

.gov    means that this is a government site. There are a whole range of extensions to the domain name (these are called Top Level Extensions), e.g.:

.com    commercial
.edu    education institutions
.gov    government organisations
.mil    military organisations
.net    network organisations
.org    any organisation which is usually non-profit-making, e.g. LEAs

There are additional extensions, which you might see:

.rec     recreational
.store   business selling goods
.info    information services
.arts    art and cultural sites

You might also come across the country codes, e.g.:

http://www.schoolname.sch.uk

Some common ones are:

.jp    Japan
.ca    Canada
.de    Germany
.ru    Russia
.us    United States
.as    Australia
.fr    France
.mx    Mexico
.ch    Switzerland
.uk    United Kingdom

The good thing is that you rarely have to know any of this. You will either know the address or you will look for it using a search engine (more of these later).

Normally the address http://www.dfes.gov.uk is called a URL (Universal Resource Locator), which is what we will call them for the rest of this section.

A couple of things to remember: URLs are case sensitive and usually use lower case only; the www part of the URL is sometimes left out.

**The browser window**. Below is the browser window for Internet Explorer 6.

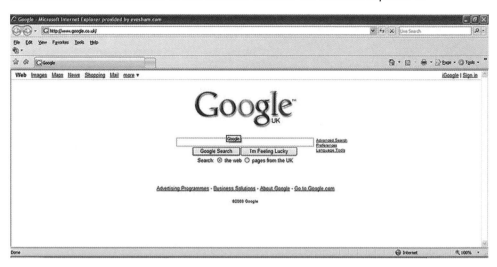

The page displayed above is for a search engine called Google. To get to this page the address/URL had to be typed into the box at the top of the page titled 'Address', i.e. in this case http://www.google. com. Pressing return or clicking on 'Go' sends the browser to this page.

**Moving around a website**. Look at the two pages shown below:

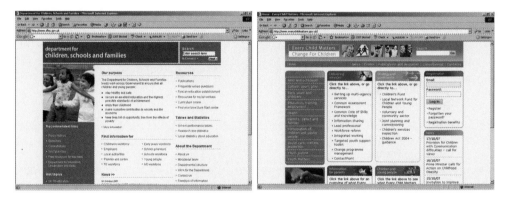

The first page is the **home page** of the DfES site. A home page is the first page of any site.

If you look carefully you will see a list of headings on the left-hand side of the page. Moving the mouse over these headings causes the mouse pointer to change from an arrow to a hand. This is a very important change and it means that the object you have moved over will take you to a new page or to a different part of the current page. Any time your arrow changes to a hand you are able to left click and be taken to somewhere else. This is called a **hyperlink**.

Try this by opening your browser and going to the same page:

**http://www.dfes.gov.uk**

Hyperlinks might be actual addresses typed on the page like the one shown above. If the link is a typed address then it will be in a different colour from the rest of the text and the mouse pointer will change to a hand as it passes over. Clicking on the link causes you to be taken to the page or site to which the address refers. Notice that the colour of the text of the address changes when you select it, and, if you return to the same page, the link you have used will be another colour – this indicates that you have used that link and visited the site.

However, hyperlinks can also be associated with objects such as buttons or pictures. In the DfES site the links are through the headings on the left. Clicking on one of these takes you to the part of the site that is referred to. Here the link to the Site Index Page has been chosen, and the right-hand page shows the result of clicking that button.

You can see the button has become highlighted, showing which one was selected. If you wanted to go further then there are various places on the index page where you might click and be taken to other pages or another part of the index page.

This is very simple once you get used to it, and it allows you to navigate around a site or move to other sites that are associated to the site you are on. In the case of the DfES site there are links to other government sites.

**Using the Back and Forward buttons**. These are useful features of the browser. Imagine that you are moving rapidly through a site and suddenly realise that there was an important piece of information on the page you have just left. Now there might be a button on the actual page that takes you back, but the quickest way is to click on the Back button in the browser toolbar and it will take you to the last page you viewed. If you keep clicking the Back button you will move back through all the pages you have seen.

You can also move forward using the Forward button, unless this is the first page you have viewed.

These two buttons sometimes do not operate as expected, so be careful and watch what is happening.

**Bookmarking a site**. Imagine you think the DfES site is one of the most useful you have found, and you know that you will be returning to it many times. Each time you could type in the URL. However, the browser has a quick way to help you.

When you are in the site that you wish to bookmark, just go to the menu option **Favourites/ Add to Favourites** in Internet Explorer 6 or the **Bookmark** button in Firefox. You are then asked if you want to add this to your list of favourites/bookmarks.

At this point you can give your favourite/bookmark a name so that you can recognise it more easily. For example, NASA (National Aeronautical and Space Agency) has a very large Internet presence with many pages of interesting images. If you have found a page with good pictures of the Space Shuttle launching, which you wish to bookmark, you might give it the name 'Space Shuttle Pictures', which will help to distinguish it from other pages of interest you might find in the NASA site.

Next time you want to go to a particular site, just go to Favourites or Bookmark, click on the name of your bookmark and this will automatically take you to the site.

**Organising your bookmarks**. For example, if you are a skateboarding teacher then you might very well use the web to look at sites on skateboarding and education. It makes sense to be able to group these. The way to do this is to create a folder for each subject. Then save or move your bookmarks into these folders. You are guided to do this when you go to the Bookmark/Favourites options.

**Using the History button**. Whenever you visit a site your computer keeps a copy of the pages in a cache, described in Internet Explorer as Temporary Internet Files. This is done to speed up access. Whenever you go to a site the computer checks whether it has a copy of this page in the cache; if it has, it loads that one instead of going to the page on the web.

Linked to these files is the History. Here your computer keeps a list of the addresses of pages you have visited. Clicking the History button will show you a list of these sites and you can usually click on the address and go to the page (which is often still in the cache). This is very useful if you cannot remember the address of a particular site and you did not bookmark it.

The computer does not continue to store these addresses forever, filling your hard disc. They are kept for a period of time, which can be specified by you. In Internet Explorer 6 this is under the menu option **Tools/Internet Options**.

**Downloading files from the web**. There are many times when you will need to download files from the Internet. It might be a newer driver for your printer, a simple freeware program or a music file. However, the most common file downloads are for documents. The DfES site, Teacher Training Agency site, Ofsted site, Standards site, etc. have all got documents that you can use. The whole of the National Curriculum, all the Schemes of Work and every Ofsted report are available, as are most other government documents.

The document files usually come in two forms, either **.doc** or **.pdf**. The first is the usual Word document file and you can load this into Word and use the contents. The other format (**.pdf**) is called a Portable Document Format file and was created by Adobe. You can only read these on the screen or print them, you cannot alter them. In order to read the **.pdf** files you will need a copy of Adobe Acrobat Reader, which you can download from the Internet.

Sites where there are programs and files that can be downloaded all tell you how to download the files. Make sure you read the instructions carefully and ensure that you get the right version for your computer and operating system, i.e. do not download a Mac version for a Windows PC.

Those sites which offer **.pdf** files tell you how to download a copy of Adobe Acrobat Reader so that you may read them.

Files and programs from large, well-known sites will be perfectly safe. However, be very careful about downloading any file/program from an unknown site. You will be offered the chance to save a file to disc, which you need to do so that you may virus scan it and use it later. However, when you try to download some programs you are offered the chance to run it immediately or save it to disc. Do not run a program, always save it.

# Searching the web

In the test you will not be connected to the Internet but you will use a simulation of a web site. This will act exactly like a real one and will include a search function.

Searching the Internet appears to be easy but the truth is that most people do not know how to do it efficiently, and end up with vast lists of pages containing information that appears to have little to do with their original search. If you use the Internet for researching information for your professional work you cannot afford the time to scan thousands of pages in the hope that the gem you seek is hidden there.

You need to develop your search techniques to ensure that you get closer to pages containing the information you require. You will be expected to do a search in the test to find a specific piece of information. To do this you will need to refine your search. You can practise your search techniques by using the Internet.

There are three main ways to search:

**Go to a 'portal' site**. These are sites that have gathered together the addresses of sites and placed them into broad categories according to their content, e.g. finance, education, health and medicine, etc. These broad categories are then subdivided into further categories, e.g. education, primary. There might then be further subdivisions leading you down through the choices to pages that might contain information you require. Most portal sites also contain a search facility for their site. Yahoo! is a good example of this kind of site, and the BBC site also has a wide range of links to other sites connected to broad categories.

**Use a search engine**. These are sites such as AltaVista, Google and Webcrawler. You type your search into the search box and set the search engine going.

This does not mean the search engine then proceeds to connect to every site and search the millions of web pages for words that match your request.

The search engines perform two actions in order to allow you to access the web. The first is to send out a small program that runs through the web looking at the pages stored. These have many names, e.g. web robots, web spiders, etc. What they do is to look at each page and scan the information in the 'META' tags. You will never see these tags but this is where the page author has placed key words to describe the content of the pages, e.g. education, primary, science, water. The web robot picks this up and sends this back to the search engine. If there is no information in the 'META' tags it quickly scans the page looking for key words to use.

If you want to see the content of a page's META tags then go to View/Source in Internet Explorer 6, scroll to the top of the page and look for the META tags.

The reason why there are different search engines now becomes apparent. Each uses a different kind of web robot program and it is the efficiency and accuracy of these combined with how the search engine software handles the next step that decides how well the search engine fulfils its function.

The next step for the search engine is to take the information from the robot programs and index this, using specially written indexing software. It is these indices that are searched when you place your search request in the box.

**Use a metacrawler**. Metacrawlers are basically search engines that search other search engines; examples of these are Ask, Dogpile, etc.

Once you have used a search engine you might get to a site, e.g. if you entered 'BBC' you would reach the BBC home page, and find another search function which just searches the local site (this will only happen if you reach a site rather than an individual page in a site).

The searching techniques outlined below should work in any of the search functions.

Although you do not need to know all the above to work on the Internet, it is useful to have some idea of what is going on in the background.

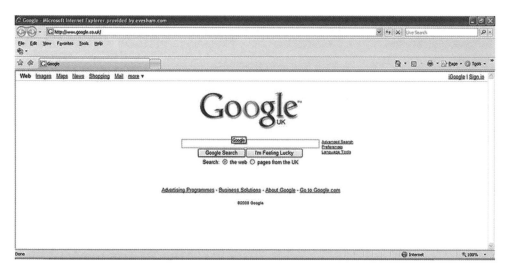

Here is the Google search engine. You can see the search input box. It is here that you enter your search criteria. You need to visualise the web as a large, free text database. In many ways you can use the same search ideas that you would use in a normal database.

The results of your search will be displayed in order of confidence ranking, i.e. how certain the search engine is that the page matches your criteria. If you are searching a single site, e.g. DfES site, then you will not get a very large list, but it will still be ranked.

## Search techniques

① Use nouns in your keywords, e.g. **education, primary, science**, etc. Verbs, adverbs, etc. are usually thrown away by the search engine. Some, like Ask, try to convert a sentence, e.g. **find me a primary science lesson plan for change in materials,** into a search string but usually they strip out everything except the nouns and work from there.

② Try to keep to lower case. Some of the search engines have limited case sensitivity, i.e. they are case insensitive in lower case but if you type the words in capitals, or some capitals, then some, but not all, search engines will search for an exact occurrence of the word.

**❸** Use several keywords. Start with the main classification and work down, e.g. **education, primary, science, materials, change, lesson, plans**. This will produce most of what you want. Although you will get many less related hits it will reduce the number of spurious ones.

**❹** You can use wild cards to get incidents of words in different forms, e.g. **teach\*** will find incidents of teach, teachers, teaching. Not all search engines give you this option (for example, it does not work in Google).

**❺** Where keywords are associated then place them together in quotes, e.g. **"primary teaching"**, **"paper cup"**. This will force the search engine to find an exact match and will narrow the search.

**❻** You can use the symbols '+' and '-' which mean **required** or **prohibited** to the search engine.

For example, **+"primary science" + materials** tells the search engine that both must be present.

Let's suppose you are interested in pets but you already know about dogs, and you realise that there will be thousands of sites about dogs which you do not want to go through. Using the search string below you can make sure that you do not get pages about dogs, but do get all other pages about pets.

**+pets –dogs**

## Advanced searches

The above all work with the simple search options. Some search engines allow you to put advanced searches directly into the search box, others require you to go to a special advanced search page and others (like Google) offer limited advanced searching.

The advanced search techniques use Boolean operators: OR, AND, NOT. These are very useful to refine searches. The test will allow you to use either **AND** or '**+**', **NOT** or '**–**' and **OR**.

**Note:**  *The '+' and '–' operators are called 'implied Boolean operators' and their use is now very common and is likely to become a kind of standard for searching rather than full Boolean.*

**Note:** *Search engines usually take a space to be an OR operator. If this does not suit your purpose then you must specify the operator you wish to use.*

**❶** Use synonyms with OR to help the search engine find other occurrences, e.g. **teach\* OR "learning about"**. Remember that search engines usually take a space to mean an OR.

**❷** You can link things together using the AND operator, e.g. **"primary science" AND materials**. This forces the search engine to include both concepts in the search so that only pages with primary science and materials will be shown. Unfortunately this will also produce pages giving 'Materials you can use in Primary Science' rather than just primary science ideas for investigating materials.

❸ Combine things together and place the main subject first, e.g. **"primary education"
AND ("lesson plans" OR ideas)** will force the search engine to pick all pages including
primary education, then any with ideas or plans, thus covering two possibilities. Note
the use of parentheses. Without the brackets the search engine is likely to find primary
education and lesson plans plus pages with ideas (about anything).

❹ The NOT operator is also very useful in excluding areas you do not require, e.g. **pets
AND NOT dogs**.

❺ One last idea is the use of parentheses to force the search engine to do things in a
particular order, e.g. **("solar system" OR "astronomy") AND Mars**. Here the search
engine will search for all pages matching the criteria in the parentheses and then
continue searching these pages for the ones which mention Mars.

In the test you will be required to perform a simple search which will mostly use the '+' and
'–' required and prohibited terms. However, you need to be aware of the other ways of
searching and to practise these for your own benefit. The test might include the OR criteria,
e.g. **+primary +classroom +minibeasts OR +insects**. Try this.

**Note:** *Many of the search engines do not respond to all these ideas so the results can vary.
Most search engines offer advice and help with searching. The test will respond to
'+' and '–', the use of quotes for phrases, e.g. "Schemes of Work" +science. These
also work with almost all the search engines and will be the first thing to try when
searching. You will only need the others if you cannot sufficiently refine your search.*

# Using images

The Internet is a rich source of images for use in preparing resources for lessons. If, as you
move the mouse over an image, the cursor changes to a hand, then clicking on the image
will take you to a larger version of that image. To use an image, just right click on the
largest version and go down to copy. This copies the image to the clipboard and it can now
be pasted into any application, e.g. Smart Notebook, Word, etc.

Two notes of caution. Firstly, some images are protected so that you cannot download them
– all images will have some degree of copyright so they cannot be used in your own
publications. Secondly, it is unwise to search for images on a whiteboard with children
present, as the search engines cannot distinguish between appropriate and inappropriate
content.

## Self-assessment questions

Consider the following self-assessment questions. These questions are intended to help
you think through what you have learned in this chapter. Can you:

1. type in a URL to find a specific website?
2. use a search engine to find specific information?
3. add a site to favourites?
4. create a new folder in favourites?
5. download updates and utilities from the web, e.g. Adobe Acrobat Reader, Flash
   updates?

# 6 | Presentation software

## Introduction

Presentation software has been available for computers for some time. However, it is the development of the digital projector that has brought them into the area of common use. Basically these are programs that allow you to develop a series of slides, which can be linked in a variety of ways. Each slide can contain text, images, video and sound. Some specific features can be animated to help focus the attention of the audience.

The most common educational use is in lecturing, in-service training and demonstrations for selling purposes. The growing availability of digital projectors in schools has meant that teachers now have access to this technology and are beginning to use it as a means of supporting classroom delivery.

The main and most common program is Microsoft PowerPoint. This is relatively simple to use and it is easy to create complete and effective slide shows quickly. Pupils, to build multimedia presentations, often use PowerPoint in school. There are more advanced programs that will allow you to create very complex effects.

The visual impact of these programs is such that there is a danger of the 'medium becoming the message'. Content is the critical component, not the number of different slide transition effects that can be included in one presentation. Indeed it is important to keep the style of presentation clear, simple and uncluttered if you wish your audience to absorb the information and not be overwhelmed by the effects.

The inclusion of presentation software in the ICT test shows its growing importance as a pedagogical tool.

It is well worth learning how to create your own presentations. Most programs have fast-track methods, through templates and wizards, which means that you can roll out your first slide show with few additional skills being required.

The majority of the skills you will require to work with presentation software are the same as those you use with a word processor. The test will only ask you to do some basic operations on an existing slide show, not create one from scratch. However, for your own professional use you should be able to do this.

## Basic skills

In this chapter we will look at the tools you need to understand in order to work in a presentation graphics environment. There will be other, more advanced tools, which you can learn as you progress but which are outside the scope of this book.

Remember that, for the sake of your audience, design is an essential feature of presentation. The templates and wizards are a good starting point for you to examine different styles that might be appropriate to your content. Often institutions develop a 'house style' using specific fonts with set sizes for headings and body text, colour schemes, logos, etc. The test uses an activity that combines all the elements of ICT within a coherent framework; this might also include ensuring that any text, etc. you create on a slide follows the style set for the overall task.

The actual operations you will be required to perform during the test are quite simple and, provided you have practised, will be easy to achieve in the time frame of the whole test.

**Creating a presentation**. You will not be required to create an entire presentation in the test but you will need to be able to do this to practise for the test. This is just the same as starting a new document in a word processor. You will be offered a start-up wizard showing a variety of templates for you to use or you can choose to start with a blank slide. As usual you can trigger this off using the menu system **File/New**.

You can create a slide master that then acts as a template for all other slides in the presentation. This is very useful because if you want to change any particular feature such as title font size then all you have to do is change the slide master and all other slides (including new slides) will be changed.

When you have created your first slide you will be in the single slide view.

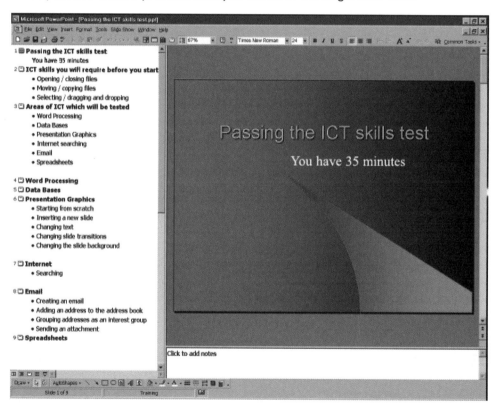

In this example you can see a slide using a 'Training' template in PowerPoint. On the left you can see the list of slides that have been created. They are in various stages of editing. Not all software will show this particular view but all will show the single slide view to allow you to edit the slide.

**Changing slides in a presentation**. It is very useful to be able to view thumbnails of all the slides in your presentation. This allows you to edit the order of slides, delete or insert new slides.

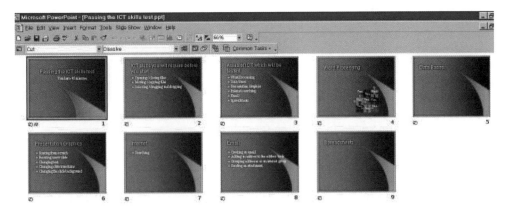

The example above shows all the slides in the slide show. From here, slides can be selected. This is done by clicking on a particular slide, using the left mouse button.

Using the menu or icon bar, you can delete or copy a particular slide. You can also pick up a slide and move it to a different position.

Note that many of the menu commands and icons are the same as those for word processing, etc. There are specific tools for this program but these are relatively easy to learn.

Practise all these editing features for a slide show. Any one could crop up in the test.

**Inserting a new slide**. This is an important tool. Select a slide as described above. Go to the menu item **Insert/New Slide**. The test will then allow you to choose where the new slide will appear, e.g. before or after the currently selected slide. Note that this is not the case for PowerPoint, which will always insert the slide to the right of the selected slide, unless you click between two slides, in which case the new slide will be inserted at that point.

**Editing your new slide**. There are no new skills here. What you can do in a word processing document you can also do in a slide, the main difference being that the text will only appear in a text box. This allows you to select the whole text box and resize it, delete it and move it around.

Insertion of graphics, formatting of text, etc. is very much the same.

In this example you can see the text box faintly outlined with the eight control points.

The text 'Spreadsheets' has been selected and a new font is being chosen using the font selection from the toolbar.

All other text-formatting facilities are available, e.g. bold, size, bullets, alignment, colour, etc.

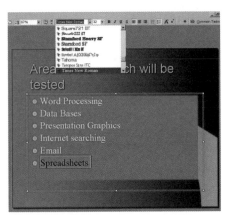

**Inserting text**. This is just a reminder of skills you already possess. Obviously text can be typed directly into the text boxes. The most important point to remember is that you can select and copy text from virtually any source, i.e. an Internet page, e-mail, word-processed document, etc. You might be asked to do this in the test so practise opening a document, marking a selection of text and copying this into the clipboard. Open your presentation and click inside the text box where you want the text to

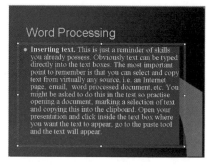

appear, go to the paste tool and the text will appear. The illustration above shows text from this document inserted into a slide from the presentation.

**Slide transition**. If you make no specific choice then as you move between slides in your slide show they will appear straight on to the screen. To make life more interesting, all presentation software allows you to change the way slides appear. You can have them slide in from the edges of the screen, dissolve on the screen, fade, appear as though blinds have been pulled apart, etc.

In the test you might be asked to alter the transition of a particular slide that you have inserted or to change the transition for all the slides. You will have a limited choice. In PowerPoint the slide transition option is found under **Slide Show/Slide Transition**.

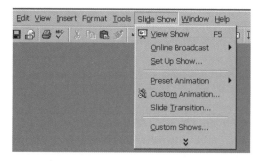

In PowerPoint you then get a floating dialogue box to help you make your choices. In the test you will get a simple dialogue box, which includes slide-timing options.

**Slide timing**. After you have finished creating your slide show you need to save it as a show. When you open the show you fill the whole screen and all the file and editing options will no longer be available. This is the version you will use for your class or audience. You have several options as to how you change slides. The default is that you press a key on the keyboard or click the mouse and the slide will change, using any transition you have set.

However, you can automate the slide show and set timings for the slide change. In PowerPoint and in the test this option appears in the same dialogue box as the slide transition options.

If you do not set any timing then the software will default to the use of the mouse or keyboard for the slide change.

As a teacher you are unlikely to use the timed slide change, because you will need to maintain control of the presentation to match pupil response. However, if you were creating a slide show to present some information for parents or governors, which you intend to leave running, then obviously slide timing is essential.

**Adding buttons**. Another way of controlling the slide show is to add buttons to each page. These are then set to move to a particular slide. This gives your audience control over what they are viewing and allows them to choose from a simple menu. You could, for example, create a slide show that covers literacy and numeracy teaching at your school. The parents would be offered an initial menu page with buttons that would take them to slide sequences covering each topic.

Most presentation software has a range of buttons built in. You can then set up the action of the button from a dialogue box. In PowerPoint the option is under **Slide Show/Action Buttons**.

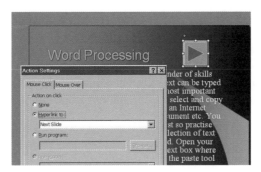

In this example a button is being inserted into a slide. You can see that the current option for the button action is to move to the next slide when the mouse is clicked over the button.

**Setting the background of a slide**. The background of a slide can be quite dramatic and add a lot to its impact.

This example shows a vivid background from Corel Presentation 9. To change the background you need to go to **Format/Background** and then make your choice from the dialogue box.

In the test you might be required to change the background colour, so just select from the options given.

HINT    Try not to select a background colour that is the same as your text colour. Remember that a bright, intrusive background will detract from your message.

**Inserting an image**. Once again this is similar to inserting an image into a document. Use the **Insert/Picture** menu. Choose the picture you wish to insert (either from clipart already available or from a file you have prepared). Click on the slide where you wish to place the image and the image will be added to the slide. Clicking again on the image will select it and you can then move it around the slide to a new position. You can also copy and paste an image from the Internet.

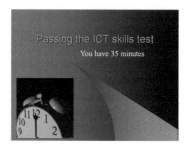

HINT   Animated gifs are great fun but test them before you use them, as several versions of presentation software will not animate them (PowerPoint 2000 will). In the example above, the clock is an animated image.

**Animation**. There are a whole range of special effects that allow you to animate objects on the screen. For example, the title in the example above scrolls in from the top of the page. The image of the clock can be made to fly in from a range of directions or fade, etc. You do not need to be able to do this for the test but it is quite useful for your own work. It allows you to make bullet points appear one after another while you draw attention to each in turn.

**Drawing tools**. All the usual drawing tools are available. Creative use of these can allow you to animate explanatory diagrams.

**Saving files**. Although this is very much the same as saving any other file, there is one small difference. Normal saving creates a presentation file. This is the one that you can edit and make any other changes you wish (you can also run this as a slide show). If you want the presentation to start as a slide show immediately then you need to save as a 'show'. There will be variations on this depending on the application you are using. This includes the ability to pack up a file for use on another computer that does not have the same software. This is done by the software incorporating a viewer with the show.

HINT   Most presentation software will let you save the files as web pages. This is an excellent way of creating material for a web site. Some animation might not translate exactly, but the latest versions of the applications create a very accurate web version of your slide show. Try this and use Internet Explorer to open the files so that you can get a feel for what it would look like on the web (some applications allow you to do this from within the program).

## *Self-assessment questions*

Consider the following self-assessment questions. These questions are intended to help you think through what you have learned in this chapter. Can you:

1. insert a new blank slide and set the background?
2. add a variety of elements to the page e.g. text box, graphics and images?
3. change slide transition effects?
4. add animation to elements on the page?
5. automate the presentation using slide timings?

# 7 | File compatibility

Sharing files with other people is an important part of using ICT to support our work. In order to do this successfully you need to be aware of a number of issues with regard to file compatibility.

It is a common occurrence in schools for staff to receive e-mails with Word and Excel files attached and not be able to open them. The same happens to students who develop teaching materials at home only to find that the school does not have compatible software to run the files from their USB stick.

Although users are beginning to overcome this problem I thought a quick guide might help everyone understand the situation and save a lot of time in the process.

It has always been the case that later versions of a program contain new functionality that is incompatible with previous versions. Thus, current versions of Word, Excel, PowerPoint and Publisher will all read files produced in earlier versions, but older versions of these programs will not read files produced in later versions.

There has always been a way around this by using the 'save as type' options in the drop down box.

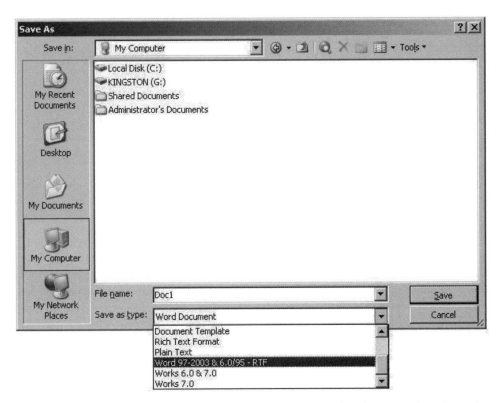

Here you can see the option which will allow you to save the document in a form that almost all previous versions of Word will open. One note of caution – any formatting or additional features you have used in the current version of Word might not be present when you save the file to be opened by a previous version.

Publisher and PowerPoint are both programs where increased options mean that previous versions of the program will not read files created in later versions. In the case of both, it is also possible to save files in a format which is readable by an older version. However, if you have spent a long time using new features, e.g. slide or object animation, which was not present in the old version, these will be lost and you will have wasted your time. If I am going to use a file in an environment where I do not know which version of Office they use, then I save the file twice, once in the current version of the program and once in a format suitable for older versions.

The rapid march of progress has now produced another issue in terms of file compatibility. The latest versions of Office – 2007 and the newly released 2010 – save Word, PowerPoint and Excel files in a totally different format, which are incompatible with all previous versions. This is causing some problems as users of these versions seem to be blithely unaware of the issue and attach documents and spreadsheets to e-mails without thinking about whether the end user has the same version or not.

The new formats have the file extensions .docx, .pptx and .xlsx and are intended to make these document types use a more open standard that is internationally accepted.

If you are the lucky owner of these new Office suites then you can use the 'save as type' option to allow users of older versions read your files. In Word this would be as a Word 97-2003 document as shown below.

Here are images from Excel 2007, Publisher 2007 and PowerPoint 2007 to help you make your documents readable by everyone.

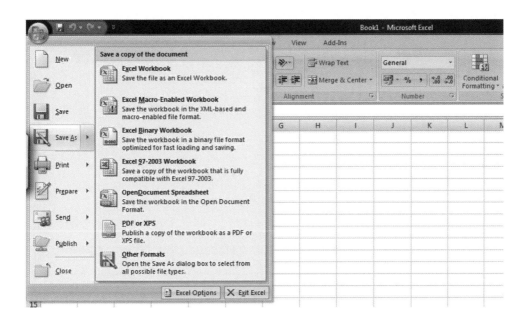

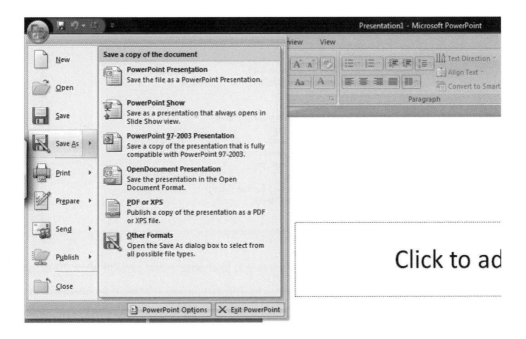

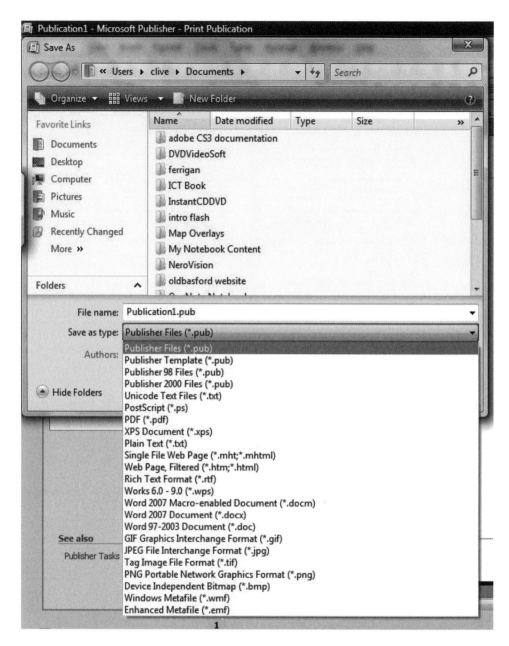

Publisher is slightly more specific and requires you to choose either version 98 or 2000 for compatibility.

For those of you on the receiving end of these files there are two solutions. You can either upgrade to the latest version of Office, which might be a bit expensive even with an Academic Licence, or you can download the free Microsoft compatibility pack for Word, Excel and PowerPoint, which will allow your current version of Office to read these new types of file. Be careful, as you need to make sure your current version of Office has all the necessary updates installed via Microsoft's site, e.g. Office 2007 requires SP2 before you download and install the compatibility pack.

# 8 | Preparing for the test

## Main menu structure

This chapter looks at the menu structure of the test. However, if you have worked through the other sections of the book, all the menus and icons will be familiar. Even if they are not in the same place, their function will be known.

Where there is something that might cause a slight problem, I have given an example.

The TDA test uses a reduced set of options. As usual, selecting some of the menu choices leads to further options. These are also simple and easy to follow. Some of the options will lead to additional menus, while others will lead to windows opening with the various options clearly displayed.

Here are the main menus used in the test and published by the TDA.

## Word processing

As you can see, this is quite simple and shows all the main options.

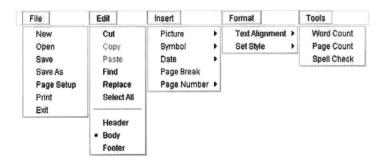

**Note:** *In most applications, the Edit menu now includes an 'undo' function.*

The icons for the Text Editor are standard and familiar to anyone using Office-style applications.

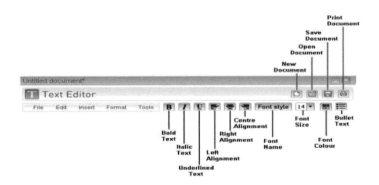

Be careful when printing as the tasks sometimes specify a particular printer, which you will need to choose, as shown above.

# Spreadsheet

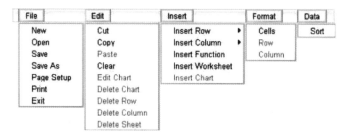

Although the options for editing a graph are shown under the 'edit' tool option in the benchmark tests, this is not used currently in the test. However, the content changes each year and this might return in future tests.

As with all applications, error/help messages appear on the screen in a central window if you do something foolish. For example, the spreadsheet cannot cope with a graph in which the data is greater than 6 columns by 6 rows. If you select an area greater than this, an error message will appear telling you what to do.

The icons offer quick routes to regularly used actions.

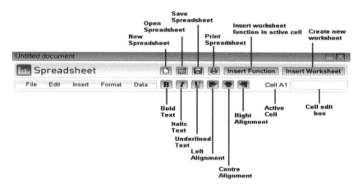

The spreadsheet has four built-in options for **Insert > Function**. These are SUM, AVERAGE, MAXIMUM and MINIMUM.

The following window then appears in which you need to type the start and end of the range of cells to be used by the function.

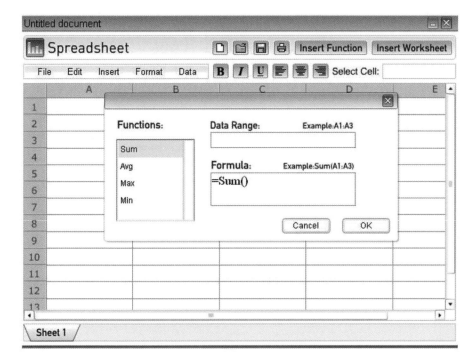

**Note:** *You may need to enter a formula, for example =(A1\*A2). This will be a simple one, so don't panic. Just remember the symbols + (add), – (subtract), \* (multiply) and / (divide). Also refresh your memory by looking at the section of this book which talks about operator precedence (Spreadsheet chapter).*

# Presentation

There is nothing here that you have not covered in the Presentation Software chapter.

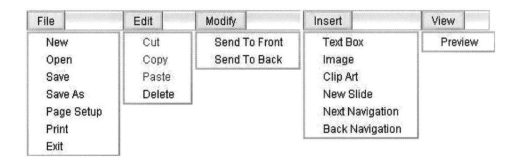

**Note:** *The 'Next Navigation' and 'Back Navigation' options under insert will place a next or back navigation button on your slide.*

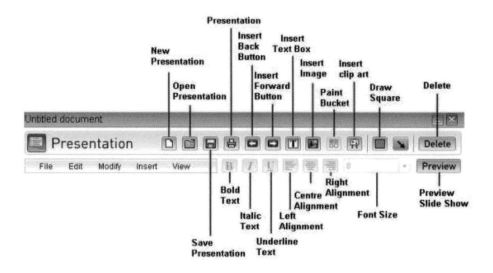

The Paint Bucket bucket icon gives simple colour options for the backgrounds of slide and text boxes. All other icons are self-explanatory.

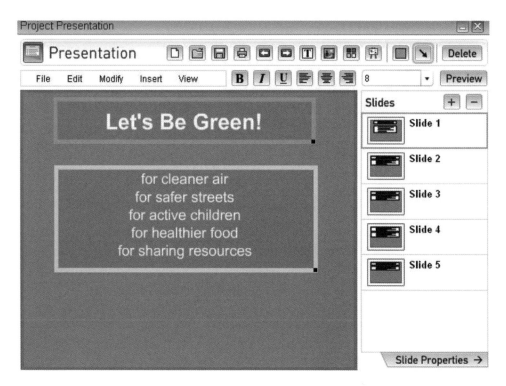

The above screenshot shows a slide. The right-hand panel shows a view of all the slides as thumbnails. Using the + or − buttons allows you to remove or add slides before or after the selected slide. Selecting Slide Properties gives you a variety of options for slide transitions or timing.

# Database

Currently this topic is not covered by the test.

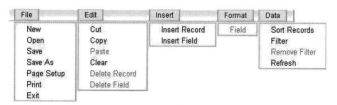

All the usual options are available. The tasks set for the use of the database are simple.

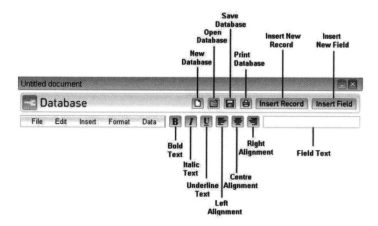

The tool icons for the database application are obvious in their function.

However, one area in which all databases differ is in how they handle filters or queries. When using the **Filter (query)** option in the test, you will get built-in criteria for the search. In the test the comparison offered for the filter is the same for numerical and text fields, which means you have to be a bit careful.

Here is an example for a numerical field.

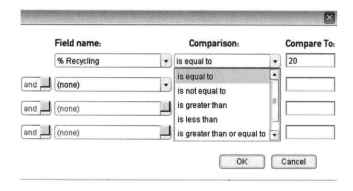

In this example the Filter is set to find any records where the % Recycling is equal to 20%.

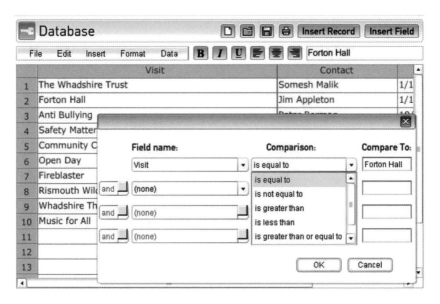

Here the query is for a text field so comparisons such as 'greater than' are not appropriate. You would usually use 'is equal to' and 'is not equal to' when creating a filter for a text field.

If you want to exclude or include data which is blank, i.e. the field contains data for some records but not all, then just leave the 'compare to' blank. For example, if you had a database for a visit and you needed to find all pupils who had not yet sent a consent form, then you will search for all records where the field 'consent form' is 'equal to' and leave the 'compare to' section blank.

If you have read through and tried out the database chapter in this book then the rest will feel familiar.

The example below is from the test of the **Insert Field** option, showing the types of field that can be created. Note the option tabs for formatting the field.

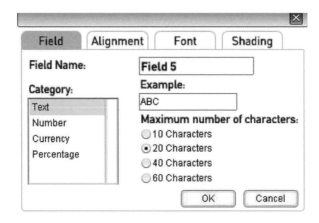

# E-mail

## E-mail messages

The menu structure is very simple and works in the same way as Outlook Express.

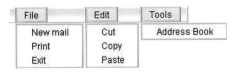

Most of the navigation around the e-mail application will be using the icon options.

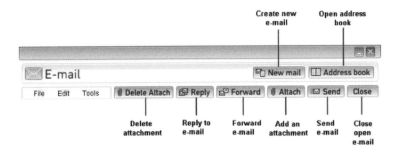

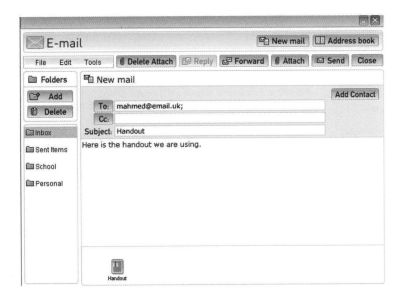

In the above example you can see that the general layout of an e-mail message is much the same as Outlook Express or web mail systems such as Hotmail. Notice that the attachment appears at the bottom of the message. Folders for the management of received e-mails appear on the left of the screen.

# The address book

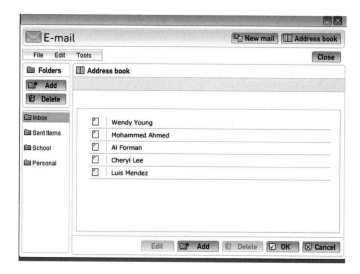

# The browser

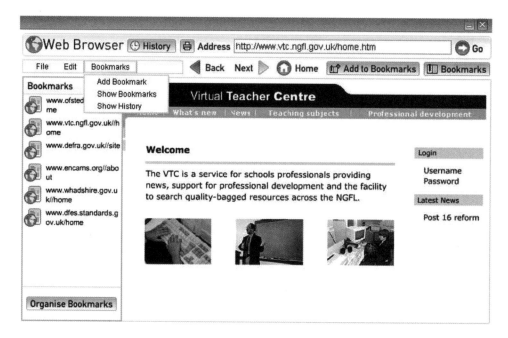

You have all the usual options, including Bookmarks. These can be organised into folders, etc.

Note:  *The bookmarked pages are shown down the left-hand side of the application window. This can obscure parts of the web page on display. Close the bookmark section when you have found the page you want.*

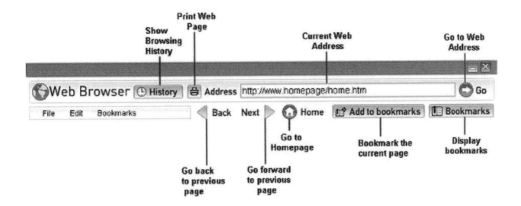

All the above tools are self-explanatory and easy to follow if you have used a web browser before.

# A few important points

The test mimics web-sites, e-mails, etc. You are not actually connected to the Internet.

Printing is also simulated.

When saving a file, choose the location given in the task instructions. If none is given, then save it back to the location where you opened it.

The files you need for tasks using applications, e.g. spreadsheets or databases, only become available to you when you are in the task that uses them. If you move on to a task and remember something you forgot to do in the previous task, you can only revisit that task after completing the final task and then using the review option. Obviously all this is included in the time allocated for the test.

All files are to be found in the desktop item marked 'folder view'. Open this and there will be a series of sub folders that contain the files you need.

# Skills checklist

Here is a checklist of 'must have' skills for the TDA test from the TDA website. Check them off and if you are not certain look them up in the book.

Don't forget that the book also contains additional skills which will enable you to practise your ICT skills.

## Basic computer skills

| Skill | Check |
|---|---|
| Able to use mouse effectively, including clicking left button to select | |
| Use mouse to drag and drop objects in applications, e.g. clipart | |
| Use mouse to highlight and select text | |
| Know your way around the desktop | |
| Be able to open and close an application which you need | |
| Open more than one application at the same time | |
| Be able to use the menu structure of a program in a Windows environment (not just toolbar icons) | |
| Be able to undo/redo actions in an application | |
| Be able to print from an application using the File/Print menu options | |
| Cut or copy text and paste it within a document | |
| Know how to find out information about a file, e.g. its size and type | |
| Understand the use of the common file extensions, e.g. .doc .txt .jpg | |
| Being able to delete files from a folder | |
| Move or copy files from one folder to another, or one drive to another | |
| Create new folders | |
| Name or rename files or folders | |
| Be able to copy and paste information between applications | |
| Able to save a file in different formats e.g. as .jpg or .bmp for an image file | |

# Researching and categorising information

| Skill | Details | Check |
|---|---|---|
| Adding an address to an electronic address book | Knowing how to use the 'Add Address' option, found in an e-mail application, to store the contact details of an individual, including their e-mail address. | |
| Adding (inserting) fields | Adding a field involves adding a new category of information to a database and ensuring that the information is stored with an appropriate field type. | |
| Categorising data into different types | Recognising that different types of data may be stored in different ways. Being able to categorise data into text or different forms of numbers (decimal places, currency, percentage). | |
| Creating bookmarks | Knowing how to save a reference to a web page so that it is easy to return to that page. | |
| Downloading files from a website | Knowing how to 'copy' files stored on websites to your own computer. You should check that you have permission to use files before downloading them. | |
| Identifying cells and cell ranges in a spreadsheet | Understanding that cells within spreadsheets are referenced by the column letter and the row number. For example, cell B5 is a cell in the fifth row of the second column and the range B5:B10 is the block of cells from B5 to B10. | |
| Internet search requests | Understanding how to search websites efficiently by choosing appropriate keywords, using quotes, etc. | |
| Recognising a web address | Recognising the characteristics of a website address, such as www or co.uk. | |
| Recognising an e-mail address | Recognising the characteristics of an e-mail address, such as @. | |
| Using the relational operator AND to narrow searches | Using AND when searching with multiple criteria to narrow a search to make it more specific. | |
| Using links and hotspots on web pages to go to a different website | Recognising a link or hotspot and knowing how to use it to go to the website which has its address stored in the link. | |
| Using the Back and Forward buttons | Understanding how to use the Back and Forward buttons to move backwards or forwards through previously viewed web pages. | |
| Using the browsing history list | Understanding that web browsers can maintain a list of the addresses of recently visited sites. Using the 'History' option to access this list and go to a listed website. | |

# Developing and modelling information

| Skill | Details | Check |
|---|---|---|
| Inserting pictures in a document | Understanding how to add an image held in a file to a text document or presentation slide. | |
| Adding (inserting) a database record | Understanding that information in databases is stored in records and how to add records and enter information into fields. | |
| Entering simple formulas, including formulas using functions, into spreadsheet cells | Understanding how to make calculations in a spreadsheet by using formulas. Cell references are used in formulas so that the calculations are updated automatically when cell values are edited. | |
| Counting the number of words in a document | Understanding how to use the word count tool to find the number of words and characters in a document. | |
| File naming | Understanding how to change the names of files. | |
| Filing incoming and outgoing e-mails | Knowing how to store e-mails by moving them into different folders. | |
| Filtering a database to display records containing specific information | Understanding how to use 'filters' to display only records containing specified information. Including using quotation marks and comparisons ('equal to', 'less than', 'more than') to specify precise search criteria. | |
| Inserting a slide into a presentation | Knowing how to insert a new slide into a particular position in a presentation. Understanding that slides can be created from templates, and how to choose an appropriate template for a slide. | |
| Inserting columns into a spreadsheet | Knowing how to add a column to a spreadsheet in a particular position. | |
| Inserting rows into a spreadsheet | Knowing how to add a row to a spreadsheet in a particular position. | |
| Moving and replicating text within a document | Knowing how to use the 'cut', 'copy' and paste' options to move and replicate text within a document. | |
| Organising bookmarks into folders | Knowing how to store and move bookmarks into different folders. | |
| Sorting database records in ascending or descending order | Understanding that records can be sorted in ascending or descending order (alphabetically or numerically). Knowing how to sort records on one or more fields (columns) in a database. | |
| Inserting non-keyboard characters or symbols | Understanding how to insert characters into a document if they are not referenced on the keyboard. | |
| Using 'find and replace' to edit a document | Understanding how to use 'find and replace' to replace instances of a specified word or phrase with a different word or phrase. | |
| Using styles to organise a document | Understanding that 'styles' can be an efficient way of categorising information in a document. Understanding that styles can be set up for different types of text such as headings, sub-headings and body text. | |

# Presenting and communicating information

| Skill | Details | Check |
|---|---|---|
| Adding a page break to a document | Knowing how to add a page break into a document in order to place information on a new page. | |
| Adding a transition to a slide | Knowing how to add a transition to one or more slides so that there are visual effects when slides are displayed in a presentation. | |
| Adding an attachment to an e-mail | Knowing how to send files as well as messages via e-mail. | |
| Adding 'Next' and 'Back' navigation buttons to a presentation | Understanding how to link a series of slides using navigation buttons. | |
| Adding page numbers to a document | Knowing how to add page numbers to a document that automatically updates as new pages are added. | |
| Adding the date to a document | Knowing how to add the date so that it automatically changes as the document is updated. | |
| Altering fonts – font size, font style | Knowing how to change the font, font size and font style used in a document. | |
| Altering page orientation – landscape, portrait | Knowing how to change a document so that it can be printed in either portrait or landscape format. | |
| Applying formatting to different types of data, including numbers and dates | Understanding that data of a particular type can be displayed in a number of different ways. For example, a number might be displayed with one or more decimal places. | |
| Creating a chart from data in a spreadsheet | Knowing how to select numerical information in a spreadsheet and display it as a chart of the appropriate type (pie, bar, line). | |
| Copying an e-mail to another person | Knowing how to copy someone in on an e-mail addressed to another person. | |
| Forwarding an incoming e-mail to another person | Knowing how to forward (send on) a copy of an incoming e-mail to another person. | |
| Labelling a chart | Understanding how to add labels to a chart to improve the presentation. | |
| Saving an e-mail attachment | Knowing how to save a file that is attached to an incoming e-mail. | |
| Replying to an e-mail | Knowing how to reply to an incoming e-mail. | |
| Sending an e-mail | Knowing how to create a new message and complete all the sections. This includes understanding the 'To' and 'Cc' fields and using the e-mail address book. | |
| Sending an e-mail to more than one person | Knowing how to put more than one address into the 'To' or 'Cc' sections of a message. | |
| Setting the background colour of a slide | Knowing how to set the background colour of one or all slides. | |
| Text alignment – left, right and centre | Knowing how to align text to either the left, right or centre of the whole or a section of a document. | |
| Using styles to alter the presentation of a document efficiently | Knowing that using styles is a fast way of ensuring that a document is presented consistently. | |
| Using timers in a presentation | Knowing how to add a time delay between slides to automate a slide presentation. | |

# Taking the test

I have tried to include some hints on how to approach the test in the various sections of this book. The most important message is not to take your ICT skills for granted. Go through the skills checklist and make sure you can do everything that is required. Making sure means actually checking by using a computer, and not ticking something off and relaxing.

Many of the skills will be ones you regularly use as part of your course, others you will use less frequently. These are the ones to practise.

E-mail, browsers and word processing are common areas that you will use frequently during your course. Spreadsheets, presentation graphics and databases are, perhaps, less often used. In order to practise using these you will need to set up a database, a slide show and a spreadsheet. The book covers the simple skills to do this.

The test will mimic real life situations. It will provide a scenario that helps to link the use of the various applications together. The TDA gives the example of preparing for a parents evening for parents who are new to the school. It combines various uses of the applications to support preparation and planning for the event.

Similar ones might include planning a school's sports day, preparing for a curriculum presentation to the governors, or preparing for a class visit. In each case you will be involved in using the main applications.

For example, you might need to send an e-mail to all governors about the curriculum presentation, make alterations to a slide show connected to the presentation, use a spreadsheet to prepare a graph showing achievement in the curriculum area, edit a hand out which will be given to the governors and edit a database of the governors by deleting one governor and adding information (address, telephone numbers, etc.) about another.

Here are a few hints for taking the test.

1. Take the practice test but turn off the clock (clicking the clock tool at the top right).

   - Look at how the test is structured, how to move between parts of a task and between tasks.
   - Read each screen carefully and take your time over the tasks.
   - Make sure you can find all the relevant files as they appear in the screen folder.
   - Try to get a feel for how long things take on the computer (e.g. open up a document, make some changes to the fonts used for titles, etc., save and close). Do this for several applications such as replying to an e-mail, altering a spreadsheet, finding information in a database, etc. Timing these operations will give you some idea of how long they take and will allow you to pace yourself through the test.

2. Now go through the test again but this time look for ways of speeding up your work flow.

   - Keep all applications open and use the tabs at the bottom of the screen to bring each application to the front.

- Don't forget that you can also drag application windows around the screen, although using the tabs on the task bar at the bottom is the best method of switching between open windows.
- Although keyboard short cuts and right mouse click menus are not currently available, note the availability of a copy button in the task instruction window. This means that if the task asks you to go to a specific web site or gives you an e-mail address you can mark this text in the instruction window and use the copy button to transfer the text to the appropriate application.
- Make sure you do not do manually anything that has a tool to do it for you, e.g. counting characters in a document, searching and replacing text, etc. The testers are looking to see that you can use ICT tools efficiently.
- Most of the applications have an 'undo' option in the 'edit' menu options, this can be useful to save time.

3. Now take the test against the clock.

Remember, the test is not intended to trap you, just to assess that you have some basic ICT skills.

Look at the TDA web site, which has more advice and practice tests for you to try.

Take your time; practise your skills and Good Luck. Remember that you can take the test as many times as you require.

## How the test is marked

Just a brief word here. You do not need to be a perfect 100% to pass the test. But don't let this lull you into a feeling of false security.

| Type of software tested | Number of marks available |
|---|---|
| Word Processor | 6 – 14 |
| Spreadsheet – where included | 8 – 13 |
| Database – where included | 3 – 11 |
| Presentation | 4 – 15 |
| E-mail | 5 – 18 |
| Browser | 3 – 9 |

These are the marks available in each section. As you go through the test you get one mark for each subtask you perform.

The pass mark is 60% of the available marks. So you have some slippage to allow for errors, etc.

# Further reading

The TDA website www.tda.gov.uk has a bibliography which points you to various training materials.

Although *Passing the ICT Skills Test* provides an adequate grounding in the main aspects of using ICT, it is often useful to have a more comprehensive manual to hand which covers more advanced usage.

The following are good overall introductions to using Office applications. Note Google Books provides lengthy previews of some books, so check there.

Weverka, P. (2003) *Office 2003 All in One Desk Reference for Dummies*. Chichester: Wiley.

Boyce, J. (2003) *Absolute Beginner's Guide to Microsoft Office 2003*. Harlow: Que Publishing.

Duffy, J. (2006) *Primary ICT: Extending Knowledge in Practice*. Exeter: Learning Matters.

Potter, J., Sharp, J., Turvey, T. (2007) *Primary ICT: Knowledge, Understanding and Practice*. Exeter: Learning Matters.

# Glossary

**Address**  An information box used in the web browser, where the user types in the desired web address.

**Address book**  Found in the e-mail application. It contains information for contacts, and is used to send e-mails without the user needing to remember an **e-mail address**. The address book can also store website addresses and telephone numbers.

**Align**  'Align' is used to move data to the right, centre or left side of a document.

**Bold**  This function is used to create bold text.

**Bookmark**  The facility used in web browsers to mark a piece of information so that it can be found again very quickly.

**Boolean field type**  A database field type used to record information where only two options are available, e.g. TRUE/FALSE or YES/NO.

**Browser**  A browser is a computer program that displays information held on the Internet. When a website address is typed into a browser, the browser retrieves and displays the information on that site, including text and images.

**Cells**  Cells are the constituent pieces of a **spreadsheet**. They can contain discrete pieces or cross-referenced pieces of data as well as formulae and text.

**Clear**  Part of the **edit** functions. It is used to clear data from a cell in a **spreadsheet** and **database**. It can also be used to clear large chunks of data by highlighting the cells and then selecting 'clear'.

**Clip art**  Small picture icons used in **presentations** and text documents. Can be inserted using 'insert'.

**Copy CC**  Used in e-mail applications to add additional **e-mail addresses**.

**Copy**  Used to copy data without removing. To be used with **'paste'**.

**Cut**  Used to remove data from a document, and can be used with **'paste'** or as a delete function.

**Date field type**  A database field type used to record dates in a certain format, e.g. DD/MM/YYYY.

**Database**  A database stores information that consists of records that contain fields. The fields may vary in type, some may be text related and others number related. Extra fields may be added to records in order to accommodate new pieces of information. A query can be made to locate specific pieces of information from all the records in the database.

**Decimal field type**  A database field type is used to record numbers with decimal places, e.g. to one, two, three decimal places, etc.

**Delete**  Deleting is used to remove something from a document.

**Desktop**  Desktop is the name for the interactive work area of your computer where files and folders are stored.

**Dissolve**  Dissolve is a type of transition or special effect between slides. It can be used to emphasise information within a **presentation**. This has the appearance of causing text or images to dissolve into tiny pieces until they disappear.

**Download**  This is the term used to describe copying files from a web site to your computer.

**Edit**  Edit is used in all applications except web browser. Facilities in 'edit' include 'cut', 'copy and paste', and 'find and replace'.

**E-mail**  E-mail allows the user to send and receive messages from one computer to another over any distance often using telephone lines.

**E-mail address**  E-mail addresses are used to send and receive e-mails and can be recognised by the @ symbol which forms part of the address.

**Fade**  Fade is a particular style of transition between slides. As the **presentation** moves from one slide to another, the second slide replaces the other one, fading over the screen.

**Field**  Information in **databases** is separated into different categories of information. These are known as 'fields'. For example, in a database used to store contacts, 'first name' might be one of the fields and 'last name' another field.

**File**  A file on a computer is an electronic document, which might be a letter, a picture, a sound, or a video clip. All files have a file name and are stored in a specific folder or directory on the computer's disk.

**Filter**  A type of database query. See **database**.

**Find**  A facility which allows data to be found automatically.

**Find and replace**  A function used to replace one piece of text with another within a document. You can either replace different pieces of text one by one or, if there are multiple corrections to be made, replace several together by selecting 'replace all'.

**Folder**  A folder or directory is used to store a group of files.

**Font**  Font allows you to change the style of the text. There are a number of different styles of font.

**Footer**  It is used to place data into the bottom of a document, for example, the page number, date or document title. When data has been added to a footer or **header** it will continue to appear in the document from page to page.

**Format**  Format is a term used to describe how information appears within a program. For example, setting cells within a **spreadsheet** to display currency signs or numbers to two decimal places, or adding stylistic effects to a word processing document.

**Formulae**  A formula or function is a calculation. In a spreadsheet, a calculation is made up of mathematical symbols such as +,-,*,/ together with references to the cells they are to be applied to. There are also more complicated types of formula such as sum and average which also use cell references.

**Forwarding**  The forward facility enables the user to send an e-mail message they have received to another person or persons.

**Graph**  A graph is another method of presenting data that is usually generated from a spreadsheet table. See also **spreadsheet**.

**Graphic** See **picture**.

**Header**  Similar to a **footer** but used to place data at the top of a document.

**Highlight**  Highlighting refers to the action of selecting an object or piece of text by using the mouse to click, drag and release it to mark it. Subsequent actions then apply to the object or text marked.

**History**  The history facility in web **browsers** allows you to revisit web sites you visited on previous occasions but forgot to bookmark. Usually the addresses of these locations are stored for a set period of time before they are removed from the browser.

**Hyperlink**  Hyperlinks are links within text which connect to other text, pictures or multimedia objects. They are usually found within web sites and connect different web pages.

**ICT**  The acronym for information and communications technology.

**Image** See **picture**.

**Insert**  The options available in insert differ for each application. In text editor, it is used to insert a picture file, the current date, page number, symbol and a page break. In **spreadsheet,** it is used to insert columns, rows, functions, charts and worksheets. In **database**, it is used to insert a new field or record. In presentation, it is used to insert a text box, an image, a new slide, clip art and a next or previous slide button.

**Landscape**  Landscape is a paper orientation. It allows data to be printed on a wider area of space, whilst reducing the length, as opposed to the default setting of **portrait**.

**Number field type**  A database field type used to record numeric items.

**Page setup**  Page setup uses the same settings as the print options box. It is used to change the quality and orientation of the paper.

**Paste**  Paste is used with 'cut' to copy text from one area to another. It can be used to copy text from document to document.

**Picture**  Pictures, graphics or images are the generic names for files that are created by painting programs on the computer.

**Portrait**  The standard orientation for paper; this is the default setting for printing documents. See also **landscape**.

**Presentation**  This software is made up of slides which are essentially a platform to present ideas. It is designed to display text, graphics and other multimedia forms.

**Print**  It is used to print multiple copies of documents.

**Record**  A record is a single unit of data within a **database** that may contain certain fields of different types.

**Reply**  Reply is a facility within the e-mail program that enables you to reply directly to the person sending the e-mail without having to create a new e-mail or find the address. Using 'reply' also ensures that the original message is included within the return message.

**Save**  Save is a function that is used in all software programs. It ensures that all changes to a file are stored. Some programs automatically save information as it is entered.

**Save as**  Using 'save as' will enable the user to save a current document with a revised name or save a new document with a new name.

**Slide**  A slide is a page in a sequence of pages that make up a presentation file or slideshow.

**Sort**  Sorting is a function by which a range of data can be arranged in either numerical or alphabetical order depending on the type of date. The order can be either ascending or descending (reverse).

**Spreadsheet**  A software application, in which textual and numerical data can be entered, stored and displayed. It can perform sophisticated calculations and can be used to draw graphs of the data.

**Style**  Style is the term used to describe a combination of display attributes that can be applied to a piece of text. For example, a style may consist of a particular font in a particular size, colour and type such as italic. When a style is added to a piece of text all of these attributes are applied to the text at the same time.

**Text field type**  A database field type used to record text and general characters. The size of the text field can be defined by completing the 'number of characters' box.

**Timer**  The timer is a function in presentation software that allows the progression from one slide to another after a defined period of time.

**Tools**  The tools function is used in text editor only. This function allows the user to word count, spell check and page count a document.

**Transition**  Transition is the name for a special effect that can be added to a presentation. These visual effects can be viewed when moving from one slide to another. The most common types of transition are dissolve, fade and wipe.

**View/preview**  View and preview are used in presentation to allow the user to view the whole slide show.  This is useful to check that any editing has been carried out correctly.

**Web address**  Every web site has an address that can be used to locate it. Addresses can usually be identified by their distinctive format. For example, education institutions contain *.ac* within them, companies contain *.co* within them and organisations contain *.org* within them.

**Wipe**  Wipe is the name of a particular style of transition between slides. As the **presentation** moves from one slide to another, the second slide replaces the other one in a wipe from left to right over the screen.

**Word processor**  A software application allowing the user to enter, edit, manipulate, store and print pages of text using a computer. Modern word processors have desktop publishing capability.